LIFE
STORIES

LIFE STORIES

D.J. CARSWELL

10 Publishing
a division of 10 ofthose.com

First published in Great Britain in 2020

British Library Cataloguing in Publication Data
A record for this book is available from the British Library

ISBN: 978-1-913278-01-4
eBook ISBN: 978-1-913278-02-1

Designed by Jude May

Printed in Denmark by Nørhaven
Cover images © eichinger julien, iStock | epifantsev, Adobe Stock

10Publishing, a division of 10ofthose.com
Unit C, Tomlinson Road, Leyland, PR25 2DY, England
Email: info@10ofthose.com
Website: www.10ofthose.com

3 5 7 10 8 6 4

Contents

What Is Normal?

It all began when I attempted to compose a letter to a newspaper about something that had infuriated me. My wording went wrong in the first sentence: 'Having come from a normal background ...'

Barely had these words escaped from my fingertips when they seemed to rush accusingly straight back into my head, carrying a loaded question: 'What is normal?'

For some, 'normal' is having a celebrity lifestyle which includes a mansion and fast cars, but for others it is being a bus driver or playing sport, while for a few it is performing brain surgery. They are not my 'normal'! What is yours?

The ever-rising production and output of books, magazines and newspapers plus the plethora of television programmes, websites and social media all reveal our fascination with the intimate details of other people's lives. All the stories contained in this book are about real people. You may even recognise some of your 'normal' in their lives.

In my first book, *Real Lives*,[1] I interviewed people from different backgrounds and experiences who each had a story to tell of a changed life since coming to faith in Jesus Christ.

Many more were willing to share what had happened to them. Some of them, in the following chapters, will let you follow the twists and turns of their lives as they discover the true meaning of life and hope for the future.

1

Paul Jones and Fiona Hendley – A Blues Singer and an Actress

The blues tells a story. Every line of the blues has a meaning.

(John Lee Hooker)

Blues are the songs of despair, but gospel songs are the songs of hope.

(Mahalia Jackson)

Tousle-haired, and still with a cheeky smile and twinkling blue eyes, Paul Jones is one of the enduring legends to have come out of the sixties musical explosion. A harmonica player, radio personality and TV presenter, Paul might be more easily recognised by some from the famous bands which brought him fame: Manfred Mann and The Blues Band. His acclaimed Radio 2 programme about the R & B scene ran for over thirty-two years, serving and entertaining a dedicated and well-informed audience. Still on the road doing gigs up and down the UK with his beloved harmonica (he is president of the National Harmonica League), he will also find time to chat publically about another passion of his. Something happened to him that was to change the course of his life but not his career.

Although his grandfathers were both musical (they played the trumpet, saxophone and clarinet) and his parents took up the piano and violin, Paul had no interest in playing an instrument. Despite growing up in the naval city of Portsmouth, nor did Paul follow his father into 'the senior service'. After a spell at grammar school, Paul moved to Edinburgh Academy for his final two years of schooling, before heading down south again to Jesus College, Oxford, having won an Open Exhibition. But the academic life was not to be, as consequently he left behind the lofty spires of Oxford and chose the more precarious but exciting world of pop, rhythm and blues, bands and the charts.

Paul, looking back at those early days when the whole world of music was being revolutionised, explains:

As a member of the cathedral choir, I knew that I enjoyed singing. I really didn't mind what kind of singing it was. Two boys in the year above me, who were both music fans, recommended me buying some records by Jo Stafford and Percy Faith. Well, I didn't like that music. Instead I took home Nat King Cole's 'When I Fall in Love'. I also bought 'Because of You There's a Song in My Heart'. Sammy Davis Jr. did a very entertaining version of that, a two-sided 78 rpm. On one side he imitated singers and on the other he imitated actors. It was all uncannily brilliant. I became a lifelong fan of the man.

Along came Lonnie Donegan, who became a star with the big hit song 'Rock Island Line'. During the course of an interview Lonnie was asked, 'What on earth gave you the idea of writing this song?' In reply Lonnie admitted that he hadn't written it at all; Lead Belly had. By this time I was into jazz – Count Basie and others of that genre. Not knowing about Lead Belly, I enquired at my record store if they had anything by him. 'Lots,' they told me. So that was when I bought my first blues record and I have been a blues fanatic ever since.

Fans, including Paul, used to hang out at a club in Ealing on a Saturday night to listen to Alexis Korner's band, Blues Incorporated. Three of the people who used to go there fairly regularly were Brian Jones, Mick Jagger and Keith Richards. Charlie Watts was already in Alexis' band. Paul recalls an extraordinary conversation with Brian one day:

Brian told me that he was forming his own band and asked would I like to be his lead singer. I turned his offer down so Brian chose Mick Jagger instead! When asked if I regret that decision, I have to say that I did not turn down The Rolling Stones; I turned down a band that Brian was forming. If

I had joined the band, it would never have become The Rolling Stones.

Having watched the successful rise of Brian's band, however, the next time somebody made a similar request, he accepted. This group became Manfred Mann with Paul as lead singer. Their first real hit was '5-4-3-2-1', which was a group-composed song.

Originally it was commissioned by London Weekend Television, who asked us to write a signature tune for a programme called Ready Steady Go! *We went away, armed with all the company's suggestions, and came up with the famous hit song. Other songs followed, including 'Pretty Flamingo', 'Sha-la-la', 'Come Tomorrow', 'Do Wah Diddy Diddy' and 'If You Gotta Go Now, Go Now'.*

Before long Paul went solo – with his harmonica – as well as developing other interests as an actor. In 1979 he was to form the highly acclaimed Blues Band, which helped to kick-start a surge of interest in blues music.

Becoming an actor was the start of several changes in his life. Richard Eyre invited Paul to join the National Theatre cast of *Guys and Dolls* for a new production of *The Beggar's Opera*. Shortly afterwards he took over the leading role of Sky Masterson in *Guys and Dolls* as well. Opposite him, in the role of leading lady, was quite a famous person who then left the show at short notice.

Fiona had already been working in a West End show in the Astoria Theatre, London and auditioned for the vacant role. Her audition song was 'I Don't Know How to Love Him' from *Jesus Christ Superstar*. Fiona, 'a little pipsqueak' (her own words), asked the director for an audition at the Royal National Theatre. She was given the vacant role, beating much more famous people. 'I thought that the man I was playing opposite was Herman from Herman's Hermits!' Fiona remembers ruefully. Wrong man, wrong band, Fiona!

Rehearsals began first of all for *The Beggar's Opera* at the National Theatre. The very first scene Paul and Fiona had to play together was one in which they kissed. Fiona was so embarrassed about kissing in the rehearsals that even today she remembers the incident as being, 'Awful, really awful!' Paul's account goes into more detail about the event and the attractive woman who had caught his attention:

The scene was really complicated as far as the staging was concerned. Basically there was a sort of raid and all of a sudden the whole stage was alive with people. They kept getting it nearly right but the director would stop and say, 'Ok, this is wrong and this is wrong but this and this is right so just watch that … Ok, start again, hold the kiss! We must have kissed about thirty times that day.

Having discovered, no doubt fairly quickly, the true identity of 'her man', Fiona and Paul not only worked together but also became an item. What a whirlwind journey for a girl who didn't have the best of starts in life.

My father left home when I was about three years of age to go off with someone else. Because of this my mother had a nervous breakdown. She and I were on our own for a very long time, during which I began to be extremely insecure about not having my father's love. Mum did a great job but I ached for that father's love.

Fiona thought she was a Christian, though she didn't know what that meant nor who God was, having little understanding of Him at all. When she was twelve years old, her auntie took her to see the show *Jesus Christ Superstar*, which had a profound impact on her life – despite it being a dangerous distraction from finding the Truth, which she did eventually.

Written by Andrew Lloyd Webber and Tim Rice, *Superstar* is roughly the life story of Jesus Christ as far as they both knew it. Much of it, but not all, agreed with the Bible's account.

I was just so moved at Jesus, who went about doing good, healing people who were distressed and who were oppressed of the devil. The scenes were played brilliantly but at that time I didn't know the whole story. Of course what happened is that Jesus was arrested because the Pharisees hated him and the religious leaders couldn't stand Him.

They wanted Him killed. It was beautifully performed, with blood everywhere and Jesus Christ hanging on a cross. The whole experience never left me. But I left the theatre that night not knowing why He was on that cross.

With all the pain that was going on in her family, Fiona had, in her eagerness to understand spiritual things, gone in a wrong direction by becoming involved in the occult.

I went to see mediums, spiritualists, fortune tellers, palm and crystal readers, and anything that was New Age stuff. But it opened the most horrendously dark dawn in my life. Home life began to be absolutely awful. There were financial problems, arguments and all that kind of thing. I didn't care about school so I used to bunk off. It was all so painful. I still called myself a believer but didn't see how Jesus fitted in at all.

When I met Paul, I was still dabbling with this stuff and yet calling myself a Christian. I was as lost and confused as could be. Paul had considered himself an atheist. So both of us were far from God at that point.

While working at the National Theatre, Fiona was also doing a radio play for the BBC. After finishing this, instead of going straight back to the theatre on the tube, she popped into the church right next to the BBC because she felt an overwhelming desire to go into one. This was quite weird for Fiona, who didn't really care much for churches.

All Souls, Langham Place is, in fact, very well-known with a large congregation and orchestra as well as having a marvellously light and beautiful interior. (Spot it with its conical spire on film clips which precede the BBC news each day!)

Fiona walked in and sat down in one of the seats. No one else was there. Casually, she picked up one of the Bibles in front of the seat. Not knowing where to read, she just flicked it open and read these words from John's Gospel:

> *For God so loved the world that he gave his one and only Son, that whoever believes in him shall not perish but have eternal life (John 3:16).*

> *My heart started to race and I thought, 'What is this eternal life? Do I believe in Jesus really? Would I have eternal life if anything happened to me ... No, I wouldn't. I raced back to the theatre, knocked on Paul's dressing-room door, and told him what I had been doing and that I wanted to go to church on Sunday. Paul's reaction was, 'I'm coming with you!'*

They continued to attend All Souls but also carried on with their high-profile careers and usual sleeping arrangements.

Paul's departure from vocal atheism came as a result of his love of art, particularly the German artist Friedrich, who lived two centuries ago. Looking at paintings in art galleries, Paul decided that atheism wouldn't work. He explains:

Basically it was understanding spirituality and the presence
of spirituality in works of art which convinced me that not
only can you get spirituality into a work of art but also if I
could recognise it, there was more to me than I thought. So
atheism wouldn't work for me.

Out of the blue one day, Paul and Fiona received a phone
call from Cliff Richard. He invited them to an event at the
White City Stadium in London, with dinner afterwards.
Paul agreed, but on discovering that it was to hear Luis
Palau, a Christian preacher from South America, he
expressed 'a certain kind of residual cynicism' – especially
as this man was hoping to fill the arena nightly for a whole
month. But Fiona really wanted to go.

They had no idea exactly what to expect, never having
been to anything like it before. She recalls, 'It was a beautiful
summer night with hundreds of people – sixteen thousand
– streaming in to the venue. Did this mean people wanted
to know about God? It really impacted me.' Music played a
big part, including a large choir. Luis then got up to speak,
starting by reading these words from the Bible:

I am not ashamed of the gospel, because it is the
power of God that brings salvation to everyone who
believes (Romans 1:16).

Luis explained in simple terms what that gospel, or good
news, really is. Jesus, God's only Son, came into the world

because God loves us and wants to restore us into a right and loving relationship with Him. Our relationship is broken because our sin cuts us off from God. The only way to restore it is by someone who is perfect dying in our place as a substitute. Only Jesus could fulfil this. He died on the cross, paying the penalty for the sin of the world. Then He rose from the dead as living proof that He was fully God and fully man. Through Jesus we can receive forgiveness for our sins and eternal life – a home in heaven with Him.

Fiona responded in this way: 'When I heard about this love and forgiveness and eternal life, I stood up. I was prepared to go along with others to the front as a public witness to the fact that I wanted to receive Jesus Christ as my Lord and Saviour, and help in knowing more.' There then followed the most amazing, life-changing set of circumstances, and a curious dialogue between celebrity actor and actress.

Paul grabbed her arm: 'Where are you going?' Fiona replied, 'I am going to do just what he said and give my life to Jesus.' Paul retorted, 'Great! Where am I sleeping tonight?' There was a long pause then Paul asked, 'Will you marry me?'

Paul shares what was going on in their hearts and minds in those precious moments:

You've got to understand that for me it was a double problem. Firstly, I had been an atheist for twenty-five years and a very noisy, vocal one at that! I thought, 'I can't walk down there; people will laugh at me.' That was pride that had to go. I was kind of embarrassed and I didn't want to commit then. So Fiona's responding and I'm not. Then here comes the other part of the problem: where am I sleeping tonight? We were going to church but living together. We were getting away with that but at our loss. Fiona's response was brilliant: that our sleeping arrangements were a very insignificant matter that would sort itself out rapidly; that we would be absolutely insane not to take this opportunity tonight while it is right there in front of us. Meanwhile the meeting is carrying on all around us and Luis is speaking at the front.

Fiona continues:

I had been terrified of marriage – really terrified. Seeing my mother go through two very bad marriages and then knowing that Paul had been married and divorced years before made me wary. But I knew I loved this man so much. There was a pause in our conversation and then when he asked me to marry him, all my fears left me. I thought in those moments how we were going to come under the cover and protection of this wonderful God that I had just heard about. I knew it would be alright. I need not be afraid. I looked back and said to Paul, 'Yes, yes, yes!'

That night we both made a commitment to God and to each other. Despite Paul's initial fear and pride, we both prayed to ask Jesus to forgive us and be our Lord and Saviour. We both left the stadium so filled with joy. There was a sense of being cleansed. When you say, 'Jesus, forgive me,' you don't realise how powerful that is and how different you will feel afterwards. We then went out for dinner, grinning from ear to ear.

Thirty or so years on, Paul is still in the entertainment world, expressing his passion and talent for music. He also spends much of his time 'on the road' with Fiona, sharing publicly – in the media and on television, as opportunities occur – the good news of Jesus Christ. Reading the Bible, God's Word, and prayer have become very much part of their lives and a source of great strength. 'Celebrity status is dangerous,' reminds Paul. 'The adulation that is received is one of the worst drugs. It is pretty much as bad as heroin and it has very much the same result ... dead rock stars.'

Paul and Fiona know that, despite the accolades from the world, their true identity is that they are each a child of God. They are known to Him and are loved dearly, not because of who they are or what they have accomplished, but because of what Jesus has done for them.

2

Sarah – A Police Officer

The role of the police service is to uphold the law
fairly, and firmly; to prevent crime;
to pursue and bring to justice those who break the
law; to keep the King or Queen's peace;
to protect, help and reassure the community;
and to be seen to do this with integrity,
common sense and sound judgement.

(Police Studies Institute)

The television scene slowly built up an atmosphere of suspense, accompanied by sinister music, as a uniformed police officer with a torch approached a nervous car driver. What dreadful crime had just been committed? We waited and watched and wondered ... for a few seconds. 'There are cows on the road ahead, sir,' was helpful advice given by the police officer! It was only an advert preceding a popular murder-mystery programme.

Not all encounters with the police are to do with crime, are unpleasant or make us feel guilty, unless we are on the wrong side of the law. Which one of us has never asked for directions or advice and received helpful, courteous answers? Or what about the many times the Metropolitan Police patiently allow their photos to be taken by foreign tourists in London? Sadly our whole world needs our police officers because our world is not perfect. Even within their own ranks, corruption is exposed from time to time, revealing that knowing the rules does not keep a person from breaking them. These men and women wear a uniform which is intended to command respect and authority. But looking beyond the uniform, they are ordinary people who face the challenges and joys of life just as we do, and are not immune to unpleasant circumstances in either their own family lives or society.

Sarah[2] and her older brother, John, were brought up in a village in the north of England, near a large industrial town from which emanated pollution of varying kinds indicated by a peculiar smell. (New laws and local regulations have since transformed both the place and its reputation.) It was an infamous village because wife swapping was on its agenda and Sarah's parents were heavily into this, ultimately leading to the breakdown of their marriage. Sarah remembers:

It made newspaper headlines at the time. I don't know what happened except that a woman used to come to our house and mum was supposed to go to the man of the couple, but she didn't. She had met someone else and eventually she left for this other person. I was only seven years old and my brother was nine.

Ironically later on in life, as a police officer, she spent a large part of her duties dealing with child-abuse-related crimes and their victims. Sarah vividly describes some of the realities of growing up in a violent, dysfunctional home:

I wasn't aware that other people were coming into the home. My mum told me later. What I did see was my father coming home and throwing his dinner at the wall. He was quite violent towards me and my brother but very much so towards mum. I think it was when he had been drinking. I remember one day Dad being at the top of the stairs trying to throw mum down. She was shouting at John to phone the police. Dad was shouting, 'Don't!' My brother was terrified, but even at such a young age he was trying to be my protector. I was really too young to do anything at all. It was like that a lot until eventually our mother walked out of the family home, leaving us behind with dad.

I was frightened about going home from school. We never felt safe. We never knew what our parents would be like; what frame of mind they would be in. They were both moody.

Dad was just violent. Once I went to ask him for an ice cream. He said, 'No!' So I asked my mum. She too said,

'No!' Dad had heard me ask her and the next thing I felt was my head bashing into the worktop where he'd come and hit me. To us that sort of thing was normal. After Mum left Dad, he was always out drinking. I remember one night he went out and told us not to cook anything. We could eat but not cook. When he came home, we were sat eating raw bacon because we were hungry. That must have been all there was in the fridge.

Because Sarah's dad didn't look after them, she and her brother ended up being taken into care and placed in a children's home. Sarah comments, 'We loved it. We had fun. It was good and we felt safe. I have since looked it up on a website and all the comments about it have been positive.'

This idyllic period of their lives was only to last six months. Their mother and her new partner came to get them, taking them to a new home, which was a pub. Sarah felt uneasy about this change as she became uncertain about the future. The two people responsible for her and her brother were heavily into drink.

Social services had apparently described me as a sad little girl. I don't think that I was sad; just relieved to be safe. But when Mum came to get us, I was not excited at all. The man she was with was not her husband. She never married him. He was nasty. He was abusive. I would wake up and then feel his hands under the covers touching me, but that is all I can remember. This went on until I was a teenager, to the point when I was old enough to realise. One day Mum came in and caught him, and told him to get out of the room. I am sure she always knew what was going on.

The whole lifestyle of the home was horrible. I remember coming home from school and we weren't allowed in the lounge because mum's partner was there watching pornographic films. He would also leave his magazines around deliberately for us to find. He would look at us strangely. Just to show how ridiculous the whole thing was, on a typical day I would walk into my mum and stepdad's bedroom to get something and be confronted by three people in the bed: my mum, my stepdad and a female family friend. Often there would be alcohol-fuelled arguments, resulting in violence towards my mum but not us. Sometimes my brother would tell me to go and stay at a friend's house as something was obviously going on that he didn't want me to see.

This horrendous situation had become 'normal' for the two young children. The only good in their lives was their grandparents on their mother's side. They were unaware of what was going on but took them out often. The grandmother, although not a Christian but religious, had given Sarah a Bible.

Through all of this, early on I was always aware of God; always believed in God. I tried to read the Bible that I had been given but didn't understand it. But in the middle of the chaos with Mum being often drunk and angry and us never knowing what we were going to get to eat, I decided that I wanted to get Christened in the Church of England.

Sarah was twelve years old. Her mother did not forbid the christening as she herself went occasionally to church. But afterwards Sarah felt still that there was something missing in life. Just about that time a Christian musical group from America visited her school to sing and talk about Jesus. Sarah really enjoyed what she heard, so when they invited the pupils to another meeting later on in a church nearby, she decided to go along. It was there, for the first time, that she heard that God loves us so much that He sent His one and only Son, Jesus, to die on the cross, so that whoever believes in Him will not perish but have everlasting life. Everyone in the world has done wrong in thought, word or deed and so is cut off from God. But because Jesus became the perfect sacrifice for our sin, we now have a way to God the Father. By trusting in Jesus, we can have access to God.

Sarah immediately responded in her heart to God, confirming this publicly by going to the front of church at the end of the meeting to speak to someone about becoming a Christian. Repentance and belief in Jesus became the starting point of a spiritual relationship which was completely different to the only physical relationships she had known as a child, growing up in a chaotic, out-of-control home. From then on she knew she could trust God completely. He always kept His promises; He would never leave her; He loved her in the perfect way as her heavenly Father.

What happened that night changed Sarah forever. But, of course, she had to return home to who knew what after leaving her new Christian friends at the church. According to Sarah, 'All hell broke loose.' Suddenly the perception of Sarah as a daughter who had never been rebellious was shattered by her becoming a Christian, throwing the whole family into turmoil. The pub clientele were a real mixture of characters of varying morals. The building is no longer there now, but Sarah remembers it as the place where her mum would get all her mates round, including several who were into witchcraft.

I'd be out at some Christian meeting and mum would deliberately get them to be in the house when I returned. They tried to frighten me. When I was sixteen, I chose to be baptised by immersion in water to declare publicly my allegiance to Jesus Christ and acknowledge His death, by which He paid the price for the forgiveness of my sins, and resurrection. Mum refused to attend. She was so angry that she arranged a séance at her house while the baptism was going on – in order to scare me, I think. But the good thing that came out of it all was that it made me realise that I was in a spiritual battle between the forces of evil and the true and living God. I was really excited by it all, especially as I felt blessed by God and protected by Him, particularly at that time in my life.

Mum and my 'stepfather' would laugh at me. But now there was no sexual abuse going on because I was older and able to put a stop to things. I could protect myself even though I was still living among people with such chaotic lifestyles. Mum was quite confused in fact – although part of her fought against me being a Christian, she allowed me to stay with my friend, Karen, so that I could join in with the church activities nearby.

When Sarah left home at the age of seventeen, life in general became much easier because she was free. Her choice of career was that of the police force, joining first as a cadet before progressing through the ranks.

It is not easy being a Christian in certain workplace environments and the police is one of those. But for me now as an adult it is not as hard compared to all of the stuff I faced at home.

After a while I let things slide a little in my commitment to God, but not for long as I received a new posting to a former mining town in which there was a small but keen, Bible-believing church. It was there that I met my future husband,

Steve, who became a very able joiner and with whom I had three children. When we were first married, Steve had to go through all the stuff of stopping me banging my head when I was sleeping.[3] He would wake me and hold me until my nightmares stopped. Eventually I stopped banging my head. We have a very good marriage that has lasted over thirty years. My brother says that he can feel really deep love within our home.

Life is full of the unexpected, especially in Sarah's job and in connection with her mum and dad.

I have always had a difficult relationship with my dad. Some years ago there was an incident involving him and an inappropriate remark to a family member. I contacted my mum to ask what I should do. She was drunk at the time but went on to say, 'He's not your dad, you know. It is some motorcycle policeman that used to call round the house that I had a bit of a fling with!' So I don't actually know who my real dad is.

Sarah's grandfather, who once was a staunch atheist, eventually became a Christian, as did her mum some years before she died of cancer. Although having the scars of a much messed-up life, her mother's final few years on earth were wonderful because she became a different person. She did say sorry to Sarah. All this came about because her mother acknowledged the wrong she had done, asking

God to save her and forgive all her sins. By the power of God she turned her life around completely.

God is in the business of saving and changing lives ... even in the seemingly impossible situations.

3

Lazal – A Female Freedom Seeker

The first step towards liberty is to miss liberty; the second, to seek it; the third, to find it.

(Leopold Zunz)

'Why can't I be free?' the young teenage girl exclaimed, but not out loud because of the real fear of reprisal. It was a sincere, inner cry from the depths of her heart – to whom? Was she incarcerated in prison, or a slave or a fleeing refugee? Who or what was restricting her liberty? Desiring freedom, she longed to do what exactly? We could be forgiven if a stereotypical picture comes to our minds right now, perhaps of a poor, unwashed, uneducated girl living and working in desperate conditions? But how far from the truth it would be.

I grew up in a really wealthy family. We children already had a nanny and other help, so my mother never had to make meals or clean our wonderful, large house and grounds that was our home. Despite both my parents coming from poorer backgrounds, they managed, through my dad's hard work and the establishment of his own company while in his twenties, to make enough money to provide such a lavish lifestyle. My dad never wanted my brothers and me to work because he told us that he would always have enough money for us so go out and enjoy life.

Lazal's[4] description of home life seems idyllic and indeed was very happy. Once she closed the door on the outside world, she describes her ordinary life in this way: 'Basically being free at home meant we always had lots of parties. We always invited magicians and jugglers to entertain our guests and different bands to play music for birthdays and stuff. I could give my brothers a hug and we laughed a lot.' But things changed once she stepped outside her home into the streets of a very large, bustling capital city. Having obtained the necessary educational requirements to gain a place at university, Lazal now began to follow a life of contrasting styles.

On the street I was arrested four times, although I had been careful how I had my hair and always wore a proper-length uniform when going out. I'd never wear make-up but 'they' would stop me simply because I have fair skin and blue eyes. This was unusual in my country because most people had brown skin and dark eyes. 'They' loved to stop me and say something insulting to me. I really suffered without any reason. 'They' wiped dirty tissues on my face while accusing me of wearing make-up. There is a special rule endorsed by the university board that 'they' are responsible for doing this and also checking uniform to see if coloured clothes are being worn. I was stopped so many times for no real reason.

I ended up crying and going back home. My mum wasn't supportive of me because she thought it was my mistakes that caused the incidents. Dad was different because he knew that it was their problem and nothing to do with me. I have always been careful not to have a bad reputation or anything that could be made into something other than it is.

Life in my country wasn't easy at all. Who are these people? What is their background that they dare insult me? Are they themselves perfect? Nobody dares to question their unreasonable activities. Authority basically lies with 'them', so ordinary families don't have much power. Parents therefore suffer dreadfully. Whether or not the state religion means a lot or a little to them is not significant; they simply want their children to be free. When things are so strict, inevitably young people are kept at home more and not allowed out. That is so difficult just because you are young. You want to socialise with friends.

Throughout her childhood, despite coming from a good home, Lazal had felt lonely.

I always wanted to know about creation and the world. By the time I was thirteen years old or so, I was asking questions such as, 'How were we created?' and 'Who are we?' Obviously, given my culture, I was straightaway introduced to the Koran. I wanted to know from it where my grandpa had gone when he died. I tried to resolve this in my little brain! I tried to learn about religion because that is where I thought I could get my answers. I tried to be a good Muslim, by praying as they do and by trying to keep the commands, with the aim of perhaps getting to heaven. In my mind I simply wanted the best.

At home nothing much was said about Lazal's change of attitude because her father didn't believe in anything. Although he wasn't really sure if it was such a good idea to follow those things, he kept quiet about it. Lazal was always confident of having her dad's support in anything she did. Her mother, while having only a little Muslim belief, was 'alright' with her daughter's increase in religious interest.

In practice, though, Lazal could not attend the mosque frequently due to the turbulent times in her country. Many stories were flying around about terrorist bombs and attacks at mosques. Fear was tangible everywhere on the streets, so she felt to pray publicly was best avoided. At the university there was a private room set aside for prayers, but this space was not necessarily conducive for its purpose as often it was smelly and not always too clean. She would then resort to private prayer at home.

The desire for miracles was another aspect of her daily life.

My mum and my aunt would tell me that they had seen so many things, and also in their own lives, which they believed were miracles. I really wanted to see them too because they are a big thing in Islam. Seeing a miracle means seeing the power of your god, the power of your prophet. It is attractive. Whatever you want to achieve, you ask your god. But it takes a long time for him to answer, so basically people instead turn to magicians, who are very popular. For example, if a woman likes a guy who is married, she would ask for magic so that the couple would be separated and she could get the guy. These magicians are well-paid clowns who use the Koran and repeat so many things in the name of Mohammed, many other prophets and Allah to do their magic, and it works.

I've seen this with my own eyes. I wanted so many things in my life that my friend and I went straight to the magicians. They gave us lots of medicine to take twice a day. I was also asked to do some sacrifices, so I killed a chicken or a lamb. I could ask for anything, such as to gain success in a university course or about relationships. I was amazed but excited that I could get anything and everything I wanted. Yet I was so afraid too that someone else would do the same to me. It seemed that the god of that religion did not have the power to stop those things.

Real fear took hold of Lazal's life. Although she was diligent with her religious duties, she was always scared that if she was in any way negligent or careless, her god would not take care of her. She was so afraid that she actually thought that she was going to hell rather than heaven. Questions filled her mind, but there was no one she dared ask. She knew that she would be advised to be accepting of this as very few people go to heaven anyway; there could be no hope or certainty about it. With regard to life and what happened after death, she had no peace or assurance, only dreadful fear.

To go to university in her land was something to which girls aspired as it brought prestige and honour to both family and country. Most girls would bypass mechanical engineering as they would find themselves alone in a class of guys. Instead they would choose subjects such as biology or chemistry. Firstly, a very difficult entrance exam had to be faced, so prospective students would need to really work hard at their studies. If they were successful, they would face many more years of the same intensity and workload. There would be no time for hobbies. Pressure was on them not only to spend every waking moment in academic studies but also morally – girls were encouraged to sleep with their lecturers to increase their grades. Lazal battled along with all these issues but finally she was able to graduate from university, moving on to study for her master's degree. There was yet another difficult entrance examination to be faced first but again she did extremely well, gaining a high ranking out of all who had taken part.

I was so excited at what I had achieved. But my dad had had enough. He had seen all the things I had been through: the college people who had arrested me in the street for nothing; all of the stresses. It was bad for my dad, and not good for his business or his reputation to have a daughter who had been arrested four times. Actually it was my dad who forced me to leave the country to go elsewhere to further my education and job prospects. My two brothers had already emigrated with his consent. For me this was a huge step as I had never stayed overnight away from home, not even at my aunt's house. I was so scared. Tears came often. Eventually I accepted the decision as I knew it was the only way to experience freedom without stress and peace as a young person.

As you can imagine, suddenly life was very different as soon as Lazal passed through passport control into a new environment that was to be her home for many years. All her life she had known a wonderfully secure family life where she was never in want for anything and was even looked after by a nanny. Now there was no one to wash her clothes, no one to cook for her and no one to make her bed. From day one she had had to enter a different student world in her new culture, learning new skills, a new language and new customs. But above all she was euphoric with the heady new experience of freedom.

I could feel myself laughing inside as I walked the streets without the fear of being arrested. No one told me what to wear. People seemed to like me. It was normal to give and receive compliments, rather than that getting you in trouble (or worse). Alongside studying at my new university, I found a job that would bring me into contact with local people in order to enhance my language skills. I was a sociable type so my time in that city was a really great experience. I made lots of friends.

For a short period of time Lazal shared a flat with her brothers. It was good, she felt, for her to have them around. Later she lodged with a local family in order to help her adjust and also understand culturally and practically what it was to live in the city. To further her studies she needed eventually to move to a different university. She ended up in a place that was not her first choice. But the city was much smaller, quieter and in a more affluent setting, which suited her because of her upbringing during her earlier years. Lazal recalls:

I fell in love with that place immediately! I did really well in my subject as well, ranking in the top ten. Among the people I first met there was a guy called David who was in the year above me. I really valued his friendship but he questioned me about my beliefs. He asked me if I was a Christian. I responded by saying that I was a Muslim and proud of it.

Lazal discovered that actually David knew a lot about the Koran, although he himself was not a Muslim. Their friendship, while growing as they also were studying the same subject, was peppered with discussions about her religion and her holy book. Some of the things that David was telling her about the Koran were troubling. She was shocked. She decided that she would go back and read her holy book thoroughly so that she could deal with his arguments.

I told him that I would gather all my knowledge of my book and then I would defeat him and prove that my book was better than his. That happened but then he responded by saying something about the Bible. I'd never heard of such a thing in my life. I countered him by saying that my book was written by my prophet and that he was an angel of God. That was when I decided to read both the Koran and the Bible so that I could defeat David's arguments and have a good answer for him. I became all consumed with the desire to know who God is.

My first impression of the Bible was that it was so complete. Even though I had read the Koran four times, I could not get full information about it. One reads only very brief things in it; you then have to go to your Muslim leader who will explain the whole thing. But where does he get his information from?

I decided to meet with some strict learned Muslims to get answers for all my questions. I wanted to know more about Mohammed and some things in the Koran. 'Stop right there,' was their response straightaway. 'You are going to hell already. You cannot question the Koran. You cannot doubt the Koran. Tell David that your book is complete.'

But I wanted proof now. I wanted answers but they could not give them. I was so disappointed. For the whole of my life I had had the Koran but I was unable to explain it to someone. I couldn't even prove it.

I couldn't understand how it was possible that 600 years after the Bible was written a totally new guy came (Mohammed) and yet there is nothing about him in the Bible. Surely if that was to happen, there should have been some warning? The thing that really took my breath away was when I saw at the end of the Bible that Jesus said He was 'the Alpha and the Omega; the First and the Last; the Beginning and the End' (Revelation 22:13). I was so confused because I knew that I'd been taught that Mohammed is the end. But then if the Bible came before the Koran and said those things, how could God change His mind that much? If God is like a moody person, then He is not perfect. So no God exists, I reasoned.

Lazal went from Islam to atheism!

All the while her head was buzzing with questions, things that didn't make sense, loyalty to her family, science and logic. Yet from the Bible, she explains, 'I got all these beautiful stories with historical locations. I read about historical evidence.' Then she came to meet up with a group of Christian students. Sitting at the back of one of their gatherings in order to watch what would happen, she was surprised when they stood up and sang.

This was very unusual for me as we never sang songs as Muslims. There were just standard prayers with standard words and that was it! We never asked anything or did anything against the rules. Then suddenly I saw everyone bending their heads down like they were sleeping on a bench and I realised that they were praying. Afterwards a guy went to the front and told his story about how he became a Christian, having come from a Muslim background.

I was furious! Inside I was praying to Allah and Mohammed about the whole situation, asking them to help me explain and prove my beliefs. But nothing happened. I was furious with the guy at the front and wanted to tell him off. He could see in my eyes the distress that was going on in my heart and mind. Tears betrayed my anguish.

I wanted to know who is the right God? This guy, S, showed me answers from the Bible to all my questions that no one else had been able to do. Jesus said:

I am the way and the truth and the life. No one comes to the Father except through me (John 14:6).

I needed some time to think. I was really tearing apart. Anyway, I just wanted to know more about the God of the Christian faith.

As Lazal spent more time with her new friends, she was amazed by their unity and love. She had never been greeted in that way before in her religion. She really felt their love for her. Shortly afterwards she came across a book about a very strict Muslim woman, Bilquis, who became a Christian at the age of fifty-six.[5] In it she shares the many questions that she had and with which Lazal easily identified. Bilquis had been hearing the same type of voices as Lazal had – frightening voices telling her that she would be put in hell. Bilquis wasn't sure what to believe so she asked God, 'God, which one is your book? Is it the Koran or the Bible?'

Lazal carefully thought about the differences.

I could see that the Bible was so complete. I could also see in the Koran many contradictions. In some verses the great prophet of Allah is beating his wife in front of everyone. He gave lashes to her because he accused his wife of sleeping with others while he was away. In the Muslim religion beating the wife is common. Also in the Koran there is nothing about Christ dying on the cross. There is only a very brief explanation that Jesus was a prophet and that He was born of the Virgin Mary.

It was inevitable that, as a highly intelligent scientist, Lazal had many questions as she searched for truth. Everything had to make sense. Out of fear when growing up, she had suppressed her questions when faced with issues of family loyalty and religious tradition. S and his friend J invited her and other friends from the university for a relaxing weekend away where they all could have more time for discussion, finding answers to questions and learning more about the Bible. She was amazed by the unity and love that these new-found friends from a similar background to hers were showing to her. When they all returned home, S and J invited her to the church they attended in order to meet other Christians of all ages. Again she was immediately impressed by the genuine love that Christians had for each other, herself and others – even those who did not share the same beliefs as they did.

More and more Lazal was coming to the realisation that she had to make a choice. She was reaching the point where she was to acknowledge that the One True God was indeed the God of the Bible. But still inside, because of her background, she desired a sign.

One night I was alone in my room. It was 3 a.m. I was greatly distressed. I couldn't sleep. I had put my head on the floor. I told God that I knew that the Bible is true. I asked the

Lord, 'Please can I have a sign? Can I have something from You?' Instantly I smelt a perfect fragrance. I just had a peace that the Lord is here; He is hearing me and He is the Living God. I was so happy that night and fell asleep!

The next evening I contacted my friends from the Christian Union at the University.[6] They were holding a curry night so I joined them. S was also there. He and others had been praying for me. I told them what had happened and that I had made my choice to follow Jesus. They prayed with me and showed me passages from the Bible which taught and confirmed what had been happening to me.

> *... if you declare with your mouth, 'Jesus is Lord,' and believe in your heart that God raised him from the dead, you will be saved ... As Scripture says, 'Anyone who believes in him will never be put to shame' ... 'Everyone who calls on the name of the Lord shall be saved' (Romans 10:9, 11, 13).*

As a consequence of her understanding and belief that Jesus had died in her place to take the punishment for her sins, Lazal was baptised as a public sign of her confession of faith in Jesus Christ. She had asked Him for forgiveness and believed that He died, rose from the dead and is alive. Lazal knew also that she had to tell her parents what had happened to her. She prayed much about what and how she would tell them, understanding that 'I will have to confess openly to them that I am a follower of Jesus. I cannot disown Him now.' Because of who Jesus is and what He has done and is doing for her, Lazal was willing to face the consequences, even though she feared for life even from her family.

My dad wasn't as shocked as my mum. He didn't mind what I did or what religion I was because he didn't believe in anything. But my mother, even though I was her only daughter, disowned me and at first would not speak to me. I felt guilty that I had hurt her and wondered if she would ever come back to me. I was so grateful for the Christian family I had around me both at church and at the Christian Union, who surrounded me with practical help and loving care to keep me safe.

Jesus says that He will never leave or forsake those who belong to Him.

Eventually Lazal's mother came round to speaking to her, only now she was convinced that all the things that had happened to her daughter were because she was lonely and depressed. Lazal was treated as though she was sick. But the family at least began to be kind again by giving her money and some support – not for her faith, but because she was deemed ill!

Having graduated as a Doctor of Chemistry, Lazal has endured highs and lows in life but continues to confess her love for and allegiance to her Saviour, Jesus Christ.

So many times I fail but I know that Satan is already defeated and he no longer has any power over me because of what Jesus accomplished on my behalf through His death on the cross. I am God's child. He is my heavenly Father and I belong to Him. What a great and amazing thing that I am the daughter of the Creator of the universe.

Further Information

If you would like more information on the topics covered in this chapter, please visit: www.jesus-islam.org

4

Professor Stuart Burgess – A Rocket Scientist

A true work of art is but a shadow of divine perfection.

(Michelangelo)

If you were looking at a class of primary school-aged children, would you be able to pick out the one who would climb the lofty heights of academia to become a space scientist? Naturally we would need more information. How did they perform in tests? Who came top? What are their interests and background influences? Stuart Burgess would not have been the obvious choice as everything seemed to be stacked against his achieving much in life. He confesses:

I had a difficult childhood. One of my earliest memories is waking up in a different bed with my cousin's feet near my face. My mother would often have to move house at short notice due to the demands of a landlord or a family problem. Most of the time I had no father at home. My mother married four times so it was an unusual family set-up, especially in the 1960s.

I remember a particular incident at school. At the beginning of one term the teacher asked me to go to the front of the class to get a pass for free school meals. When I saw the look on the faces of the other children, I began to realise that I was different from everyone else. In early primary school I attended a special needs class for children who were slow to learn to read.

The insecurity in Stuart's childhood even led him to develop a nervous stutter that made it hard for him to hold conversations. The biggest effect on his life, he feels, was being labelled as a 'social services boy'. Besides the free-meals stigma, other children noticed that he wore 'tatty' clothes, so his only friends were those children in the same position as him. Being excluded from all the popular friendship groups was more painful than his lack of food or clothing.

Although he lived mostly on his own with his mother, he actually had four siblings, but some were taken away by social services while others were always away. Everything often felt quite hopeless.

I remember being unhappy and insecure. Occasionally I would catch a glimpse of 'normal family life' by going to a school friend's house but it didn't happen that much. I don't think I knew much about the world to make proper comparisons. I just felt lost and lonely.

I had a teacher who mentioned his belief in the Bible and I had been to Boys' Brigade meetings where leaders prayed to God. If you had asked me in my early teens if I believed in God, I am not sure what I would have said. I didn't have any deep thoughts about anything. I remember saying a few prayers as a young child in my room when on my own – mainly asking for a better life. It was a case of wanting just to survive.

How Stuart was able to ever sit down, concentrate and do any study for his exams at senior school one cannot imagine. At the age of fifteen he made a conscious decision to respond to his situation by studying hard, despite the fact that he was already selected for low-performing classes where children did not take O-levels (the old GCSEs). Teachers began to notice that he was a motivated pupil, so gradually transferred him to the more challenging O-level classes for most subjects. He vividly remembers the first maths test in his new class. He was fearful of coming last so he really prepared thoroughly. Even though he had missed the beginning of the course and had no help from home, he came first out of thirty children. For the first time in his life he felt that he had acquired some status. Stuart came to the conclusion that studying was to be his only escape from his present social class. Actually he went on to pass all seven O-level examinations that he sat. When he told his mother the results, she said she had not known that he was taking O-levels!

Despite feeling that life was pretty hopeless, when he left school at the age of sixteen, he managed to find employment at a local engineering factory, Stothert & Pitt in Bath. His wage helped to pay for his mother and him to live in a rented cottage near Bath. After work, instead of simply relaxing, he continued his studies (in engineering) at night school, having enrolled at Bath Technical College. He studied very hard and achieved very high grades.

Meanwhile his employer had noticed how well he had done and had phoned Brunel University in London two weeks before the start of term. As a result, Stuart received an offer there to study engineering as part of a sandwich course; he would have a six-month work placement and a six-month university placement each year. Stuart was very surprised to be offered a place at such short notice – he did not even know where Brunel University was – but accepted the offer because it sounded like a golden opportunity to get a qualification.

I found university very tough because I was much less prepared than students who had done full-time A-levels. I also felt a lot of pressure because I knew that if I failed or ran out of money, I had no Plan B. Looking back, I should never have made it there considering my lack of qualifications.

Even though I didn't know about God, nor had I even met a Christian at that point, I believe now that God's hand of guidance was upon my career and my life.

Stuart embarked on a course of mechanical engineering, which included maths and physics plus some really interesting aspects like designing and manufacturing. As a boy he really enjoyed playing with Lego, the popular, well-known building blocks still loved by kids today and which are great for stimulating design, dexterity and imagination. So perhaps all along, in spite of his poor start in life, there was a spark of creativity which in later years was fanned to fire in Stuart's mind to design and develop things for the space industry.

But firstly there was the small matter of getting through university, with very little support. By then he had lost all contact with his mother, who was distracted by a new husband who went on to physically abuse her. In his first year he realised that if he ran out of money, he would not be able to pay bills. That year was seriously tough. Even when the Christmas and Easter holidays arrived, Stuart wasn't sure that he would have any place to go. The uncertainty must have been dreadful. He would have had little or nothing to which he could look forward.

One day Graham, a fellow student on his course, invited him to a meeting. It was about a controversial subject concerning science, God and the Bible: creation. Organised by the Christian Union (CU), Stuart found it fascinating, but did not have any particularly strong feelings about creation. However, he did find himself being drawn towards the Christian students who went to the CU. He observed that there was a joy and maturity about them that he had not seen before – something he would love to have.

I wasn't that interested in the theology at the beginning, but I was attracted by their kindness and love as they lived it out. I began attending Waterloo Road Free Evangelical Church that some students went to as well. There was one particular Christian family, the Heldens, who invited me for lunch. Of course I accepted, being a very hungry student!

Seeing the effect of what Christians believed made Stuart think that he wanted what they had. Therefore he became interested in theology for the first time. He was to discover that it was their personal relationship with Jesus Christ that made them different people. Stuart listened very carefully to the sermons. When the preacher explained that we have to repent of sins, Stuart had no difficulty in believing that all humans are sinners. He had seen the worst sides of human nature throughout his childhood. It also made sense to him that the only way to get to heaven is to repent and have faith in the life, death and resurrection of Jesus Christ. He could have felt that he had a legitimate excuse for his past behaviour not being up to the mark because of his troubled background. There was a sense that God had given him a raw deal. However, he saw clearly that no one is blameless before God. He also felt that this was a big opportunity for him because for the first time he believed he could have stability in his life. He could have hope. And that hope was only to be found through Jesus Christ.

Over a matter of months Stuart discovered not only that there is a God, but one who is interested in him personally and loves him. While reading the Bible, various verses stood out for him:

> *God demonstrates his own love for us in this: while we were still sinners, Christ died for us (Romans 5:8).*

> *For since the creation of the world God's invisible qualities – his eternal power and divine nature – have been clearly seen, being understood from what has been made, so that men are without excuse (Romans 1:20).*

When Stuart understood in his mind the truth about God from the Bible, he wanted to repent and believe, openly acknowledging that Jesus Christ had become his Lord and Saviour.

> *… if you declare with your mouth, 'Jesus is Lord,' and believe in your heart that God raised him from the dead, you will be saved (Romans 10:9).*

I realised I had no excuse; I did have to say sorry for my sins. But after I did that, the change in my life was dramatic. Suddenly I had gone from a hopeless place to a place of great hope and certainty. God had heard my prayer and by His Spirit now lives within me, giving me stability that I had never experienced before and a huge family of Christians both locally and worldwide.

I told my mother what had happened. She didn't understand but I think she was pleased because she knew I'd had a hard childhood, so she was happy with anything that had helped me. I didn't have a lot of contact with my mother after that – just occasional visits.

It was a great joy to suddenly know God as a heavenly Father and to be part of God's family in a local church. My conversion made me realise that I had missed a stable family and father figure in my life. I also appreciated that God's family is the most important family to belong to. David and Ruth Helden were a wonderful couple who showed me the love of Jesus in a very patient way. Their life and witness had just as big an impact on me as the excellent sermons I was hearing.

After my first Sunday lunch with them, I remember writing a two-page letter of thanks. It was the first time I could remember being with a normal, functioning family at mealtime, where the children had both mother and father with them. When I visited them the following week, I noticed that my letter was on their noticeboard. I also found out that their three children had been made to read the letter several times to help them not take things for granted! I know that the Heldens have prayed regularly for me since for over thirty years.

Finding faith in his first year at university was a great help to Stuart because all the time he was studying there was support from his church family and a loving heavenly Father. It helped him come to terms with the unfairness of his childhood. That didn't happen instantly, though – it has been a long process of healing that still continues today. Having a certain hope of heaven was the biggest comfort.

Home life still had its challenges. When he was nineteen, a new stepfather came into their rented cottage that Stuart had helped to set up and maintain.

On the day he arrived, he did not speak to me but told my mother that I had two hours to pack my bags and leave. I now had to find my own accommodation during the six months I spent in Bath each year during my degree. My student friends found it strange that I had no home to go to in the holidays. That was hard but I now had the support of an entire church. When I graduated, some of them came to the ceremony.

Stuart went on to work for Stothert & Pitt for another year before leaving to pursue a PhD in Mechanism design at Brunel University. That qualification set him up for a dream job in engineering – a spacecraft designer for the European Space Agency! He recalls, 'When I started working on rockets and satellites, I had to pinch myself that this was really happening to the person who needed coaching to learn how to read!' Love was in the air too when he met and married Jocelyn in his third year. He admits that having such a wonderful wife was even better than a job with ESA!

God has since blessed us with five amazing children. There is an interesting contrast here because my mother also had five children, yet I lived most of my life on my own because the family was split up through broken relationships and social services interventions. Now I had the chance to enjoy seeing five siblings grow up in a stable family.

As a young Christian, Stuart had a strong desire to reach out to children from poor areas to explain to them that there is a wonderful hope and help in Jesus. He helped to start a work in the St Paul's area of Bristol that was notorious for poverty, drugs and knife crime. Each Sunday afternoon he and others would pick up a busload of children and take them to Sunday school lessons. Most of the children were in situations just like the ones Stuart had experienced as a child. He considered it a privilege to teach such children the message of salvation from the Bible.

However, there were some scary moments working in St Pauls! I was once walking a young boy to the place where he caught the bus when he began to misbehave. I noticed that we were about to walk past a gang of young men, including some drug dealers. One of the leaders started marching towards me as if he wanted to speak to me. I was terrified. He looked at the boy and said in a stern voice, 'You are going to Sunday school so you need to behave!' The young boy was no trouble for the rest of the afternoon! At that point I realised that even gang members had a respect for God's work in the area.

Back at his day job as a rocket scientist, Stuart went on to be involved with the development of Envisat, a large earth-observing satellite that was launched on 1 March 2002 aboard an Ariane 5 from the Guyana Space Centre in Kourou, Guiana. Other challenges presented themselves out of the blue. He remembers going in to the office on one of the first Mondays after he started to be greeted by his boss, who wasn't feeling very well.

'Stuart, how long will it take you to go and get your passport?'

'Not long. I live close by. Why do you ask?'

'Well, that is good,' replied the boss, 'because I want you to fly to Holland and give a presentation on a micro-imaging

microwave radiometer.' [This was something Stuart knew nothing about!]

'Don't worry,' the boss continued, 'you can swot up on the plane and present it tomorrow at the European Space Agency's headquarters!'

That was quite a baptism of fire. Stuart must have done alright as he wasn't fired but went on to work with them for five years.

The world of academia was beckoning so Stuart progressed to do a post-doctorate at Cambridge University. He comments, 'This was quite an incredible thing to do. Was I really the same person as that stuttering child who struggled with his reading? Yet there I was researching and teaching at Cambridge University.' Humbly he confesses that he was extremely appreciative of his time there.

He then returned to Bristol University, but this time as a member of academic staff who would go on to be awarded a professorial chair in engineering design, as well as become head of the department. He explains, 'Naturally my particular interest is engineering design. I teach my students how to create things; how to come up with concepts and then how to detail and design. Mostly they want to design motor cars, but also bridges and aeroplanes.'

Stuart's life in general has become far more normal than it had been during his childhood. He is happily married with a lovely, stable family. However, because Stuart is a Christian as well as a scientist, he has come across opposition to his literal, biblical view of a six-day creation of the earth. Professor Burgess explains why he believes God created the world and that it isn't the product of the Big Bang and 'billions of years of evolution':

There are different reasons. One main one, of course, is that I believe in the authority of the Bible – not just that the Bible says God created the world in six days but that it also explains that God is infinite in power. If God is infinite in power and wisdom, He is well able to create the world in six days. I also work in an area called biomimetics, which means engineers copying designs that are found in nature. It is a field that has become quite popular in recent years. When I study trees, birds, plants and animals in the natural world, I can see the hand of a perfect Designer.

Biblical creation is quite contrary to the whole flow of popular opinion advocating evolutionary atheism, which is promoted throughout the media and educational systems of our country and worldwide. Although it is worth noting that some of the greatest scientists that ever lived – Isaac Newton, Michael Faraday, James Clerk Maxwell and Lord Kelvin – firmly believed in a creator. Professor Burgess explains:

Because people such as Richard Dawkins and Stephen Jones are very aggressive in their criticism of people who believe in creation, very few academics will admit to believing in intelligent design. We therefore assume that hardly any academics believe in a creator. But that is not true. Many of my colleagues at both Bristol and Cambridge would actually be quite sympathetic.

One reason why there are the very hard militant atheists is because they feel very threatened by the Bible and a Creator. They don't want to think about the possibility of judgement. Academics tend to follow the majority and the majority believe in evolution. They don't follow out of conviction.

Professor Burgess has decided to use his expertise in design to explain the evidence for intelligent design and biblical creation, despite abuse, attacks and ridicule. His first book, *Hallmarks of Design: Evidence of Purposeful Design and Beauty in Creation*, was published in 2000.[7] Sadly he feels that our world has adopted an atheistic worldview and so God is banned from theories of origins, despite the overwhelming evidence for intelligent design.

Stuart's career has flourished, including an interesting diversion into the world of sport. The Rio Olympic Games in 2016 was something that Stuart followed with great interest, not only as a true Brit but also because he had been playing a vital part in the design of the bicycles for the British Olympic cycling team that won six gold medals and broke two world records. Professor Burgess has won several awards and medals for design, including one from the Minister for Trade and Industry, and has exhibited his work at the Royal Society. He has enjoyed the tremendous privileges, thrill and excitement of working with space agencies and industry, and achievements within academia and for his country. But he would freely admit that nothing compares to obtaining the crown of life given to those who have faith in Jesus Christ.

5

Billy – A Former Terrorist

The best revenge is not to be like your enemy.

(Marcus Aurelius)

'Are you coming for a drink then?'

Grabbing his coat and money, the man closed the door behind him, leaving his children and wife busy with their own activities. The social club was not far and the way was familiar by this regular trek for a drink with the lads. Belfast was changing fast now that the political troubles were in the ascendency. So the man had much to catch up on before downing the last dregs, calling it a day and heading back home. Perhaps walking briskly, who knows what thoughts were in his head as he turned that fateful corner on the Newtownards Road.

His son, Billy, recounts what happened next:

Dad was returning from the social club like he always did, regular as clockwork, when IRA gunmen suddenly opened fire, killing my father instantly. Dad was not a terrorist. He was just in the wrong place at the wrong time. Our family unit found itself united in sorrow and grief, but shattered as a result of terrorism. This was right at the beginning of the Troubles. My mother was three months pregnant at the time. I was twelve years of age. Mum always used to sing country and western songs as she did her housework but now the singing stopped.

Hatred and bitterness began to grow in Billy's heart and the heart of other family members. He describes it as a tangible hatred that sought revenge. Despite attending Sunday school as a young lad, Billy was consumed by this new passion, which drove him to join a paramilitary organisation. He thought that if there was a God, He could, or should, have stopped his dad from being shot. So, Billy reasoned with himself, either there is no God or else He's heartless to do things in this way. In short, 'I was sceptical and maybe atheistic in relation to God.'

It wasn't particularly hard to join a terrorist organisation in Northern Ireland during the Troubles. Being a very tight-knit community, everybody knew everybody else, so they knew which bars the paramilitary members frequented. Billy eventually joined one. Then there was a reshuffle of the organisation meaning that he was lectured and encouraged to take someone's life. Billy admits that in February 1976 he was asked to shoot a member of his own organisation who was known as an informer.

It was believed that an informer could do as much damage to the organisation as the IRA could. I went up to the informer, looked him in the eye and shot him dead. I participated in the execution, as it was called at the time. I didn't have any arms twisted up my back; I volunteered. As a result of that incident, I found myself in the Maze prison. I was too young to be given a life sentence so I was detained under 'the Secretary of State's pleasure', which basically is a life sentence for people under the age of eighteen.

Billy was still filled with hate and longed for his release so that he might kill again.

After a few years, Billy started receiving a Christian magazine regularly. He had no idea who was sending them so he threw them in the bin. Then one day Billy had a bad headache so went over to the medical room to ask for some tablets. A fellow prisoner, Peter, was there.

I knew that he was a Christian because when he was sentenced three weeks after me, he arrived in H Block in the Maze carrying a Bible. Somewhere between being sentenced and coming back to the Maze Peter had become a Christian and was very vocal about it. He had no problem about sharing his new-found faith with others.

Because of his witness in the prison I decided to start forwarding the magazines on to him rather than throwing them away. When I was in the medical room, I asked Peter if they were getting through to him – I was in one part of the block and he in another. I told him he was welcome to them but I didn't know where they were coming from.

The medical officer looked up and remarked, 'Maybe it is God who is sending them.' I thought that I had never heard anything so stupid in my life ... especially as they were coming from New Zealand!

Hard talk is not uncommon in prison; being blunt is a way of life. Billy told the medical officer straight out that he was sceptical of God, even to the point that he didn't believe that God even existed! The officer was equally blunt by replying that regardless of whether or not Billy believed in God didn't take away the fact that there was a God. There was indeed heaven but if Billy died in the state that he was, he would have no part of it. Rather, he would go to hell. After death he would not be sceptical because then he would know God was real, as would everyone else.

Billy returned to his cell. Those comments got him thinking. They were so unexpected. Billy thought the officer might have quoted a verse in the Bible that states, 'The fool says in his heart, "there is no God!"' (Psalm 14:1). But no, this was different. Is there a God? What about heaven? And hell? Which religion is right? Certainly that trip to the medical room stirred up many thoughts in his mind.

Billy was to spend ten years in prison so he had plenty

of time on his hands to think. Prison visitors were often welcome. That is how he came across Miss Blackburn. Previously she had taught mathematics at Methodist College, Belfast but had become a member of the board of visitors at the prison. This draws people from civilian society to go into prison to make sure that it is run along humane guidelines. Miss Blackburn used to come in on a regular basis and distribute, where she could, little gospel leaflets or Scriptures for anybody willing to talk to her.

Gladys came down to my cell one Christmas Eve. After a bit of conversation, she looked at the Bible and started to read from Luke 23, the account of the crucifixion of Jesus. God convicted me of my sinfulness. (I couldn't have put it in that terminology then, but it was as if every wrong that I had committed came before me.) I felt the weight of that wrong. I felt guilty for the first time in my life. I realised that I needed a Saviour and Jesus Christ was that Saviour.

The night after Miss Blackburn had left my cell I went down on my knees and repented of my sin. I acknowledged my need of a Saviour, and asked Jesus to come into my life and make something of it. It was a wasted life that was going nowhere. God heard that prayer, answered it and transformed my life.

Billy felt no strange, mystical experience. The only difference was that he now believed that there was a God. He believed he was coming to Him and asking for forgiveness. He believed God heard that prayer and answered it.

The change that came I guess was the change in my attitude. My values and beliefs changed. I was once spiritually dead but now very much alive. The bitterness was taken away, along with the hatred. My language was cleaned up. It used to be that every sentence of mine was peppered with foul talk. All of that changed.

I certainly did have a feeling of cleanness and that Jesus had washed away everything that was wrong. I felt that I was a new creature. I felt a peace and contentment that I didn't have before. Some of these things are subjective, but when I measure them against the Word of God, the Bible, that is actually how Christians should feel and what Christians should experience.

There were a number of Christian prisoners, as well as officers, in the Maze at that time. Billy knew that he had to tell people what had happened. He couldn't be a secret Christian. Obviously there was the fear of telling people. Also he had previously thought that Peter was a hypocrite who was trying to work his ticket to get out of prison early. Billy didn't want anyone to think that of him or that he couldn't face up to life in prison or that he needed a crutch to lean on.

What I actually did on a Christmas morning was to tell the fellow in the cell next door to me. His nickname was Shirley because he always gossiped. I stuck my head in Shirley's cell as soon as the door was open and said, 'I became a Christian last night!' Then I went back to my cell. True to form, Shirley went out and told everyone what I had done, so he did all the telling for me. I just sat and waited. Everybody came and either shouted abuse at me or shook my hand. I had to wait another five years until I was released.

Billy had written to his mother explaining what had happened to him while he was imprisoned. The reply he received hurt him deeply as she told him never to forget what 'the IRA scum did to your father and our family'. However, all was to change some months later when his sister, who had also become a Christian, took their mother to church. Mrs McCurrie was to write again to Billy explaining that she too had become a born-again Christian. And she was singing again, but this time they were gospel songs.

Billy recognises that he was a bad man who had broken the law and therefore was subsequently caught and rightly punished. But many people think they are alright because they haven't murdered anyone and always tried their best in life. What would Billy say to them?

It doesn't matter what I or anyone else thinks. It is what God thinks of us that really matters and He says that none of us are ok. In the Bible it states that every one of us has sinned. Our only way to heaven is through repentance and belief in Jesus who came to take away the sin of the whole world.

Billy's life has been turned around so much after leaving prison that he has become a Christian minister. God has taken away the bitterness, hatred and desire for revenge and replaced it with His love.

The problem with prisoners and people in society is that often there is reform but this is not enough. Unless the heart is changed, you haven't solved the problem. Education and all the other things are good but the heart of the problem is the problem of the human heart.

God promises to give us a new heart to replace our hardened, sinful ones. I am living proof that can happen to anyone, even a former terrorist.

The Other Side of the Gun

A 'chance' meeting with a Northern Irish lady recently led me to discover that she had a family connection with Billy's victim. This is Jacqueline's account of the view from 'the other side of the gun':

I was twelve years old when Desi was murdered on his way to work in Belfast during the period known as the Troubles. He was not my dad but my mum and he had been together for about five years. They were engaged, planning to be married in August 1976. When Desi was murdered on 19 February, my mum was devastated. It was thought that I was too young to attend the funeral. But that evening I remember seeing his car on the television news. I listened carefully to what was being said and looked intently at the bullet holes that were visible. His car was very distinctive, being blue with a black roof.

I had been sent to Sunday school as a young child so I knew that God loved me and that Jesus had died for my sins. However, I don't remember making any sort of commitment to God in a personal way. When I heard that Desi had died, I was shocked at the news, especially how he was killed. But I was also overwhelmed with the knowledge and realisation that Desi had entered into eternity unsaved from his sins. Without acknowledging Jesus as his Saviour, he would spend eternity separated from God in hell. These thoughts broke my heart and I wept every night in my bedroom.

A few weeks later we were told by the police that two young men had been arrested for Desi's murder. That night when I went to bed I wept again, not for Desi but for those two young men. I prayed, 'Father, forgive them for they didn't know what they were doing.' I prayed that prayer and wept every night for months, maybe years. My desire was that God, in His mercy, would save their souls. It was too late for Desi but not too late for the men.

My mum remarried the following year so it became inappropriate to talk about Desi after that. Life simply carried on. Just before my sixteenth birthday I became a Christian. But I came to God with a lot of baggage that needed to be dealt with. Within about eighteen months I admit I walked away from God (though I returned to Him many years later). Back then I felt I was not a 'good enough' Christian and as a consequence my life spiralled out of control. I did not understand at the time that none of us are 'good enough'.[8]

Meanwhile the years passed by, leaving the murder of Desi further and further back in our family's memories as we carved out our own lives. But one day I was having my dinner when I happened to glance up at the TV. I was shocked to see the old film footage of Desi's car on the news. I quickly turned up the volume. They were interviewing Billy as he was being released from prison. He shared that he had become a Christian while being inside and that he intended to train as a pastor. He wanted to use his life to warn others not to get involved in paramilitaries. I was stunned. I had heard them say his name but I picked it up wrongly as Billy McCory. I remember that night being amazed. I was in total shock at what God had done. I was so thankful because He had seen my tears, heard my cries for mercy and answered my prayers.

Jacqueline went on to recommit her life to Jesus Christ in 1995 but always wondered what had happened to that guy,

Billy. Had he continued following Jesus or had he rejoined the paramilitaries (as some do)? Years passed but often she would search the internet trying to find out if he had kept his promise to become a pastor. Somehow she could never track him down. Obviously it didn't help having the wrong name either!

I suppose the chances of me finding him were impossible. However, I believe God spoke into my heart and told me that when the timing was right, he would bring Billy across my path. So I left it at that.

By 2009 I began working for a charity called Christians Against Poverty, who help those who struggle with debt problems. In 2016 I travelled from Northern Ireland to one of their staff conferences held over in England. Normally my colleagues and I would be sent to the more northern gathering but this time we were invited to join the 'closer south' staff. Having been split up to prevent 'us chatty Northern Irish lot' being too cliquey, I found myself seated at the dinner table with friends as well as workers from head office.

We were all chatting away among 500 people, so it was quite noisy and hard to hear each other. Halfway through the night someone shouted across to me, 'Jacqui, do you know a guy from Belfast called Billy Mc …?' I couldn't quite get the surname but in that moment it was as though the room just froze. I heard a gentle whisper in my ear that said, 'That's him!' I also remember thinking, 'God, if I am wrong, I am going to look really stupid.'

Her heart was really pounding as she replied, 'I don't know if it is the same guy that you are talking about but if it is, I've actually been praying for him since I was thirteen years old.' (She was actually twelve but was nervous!) As Jacqui related all she knew about Billy, her colleague shook her head in disbelief as she confirmed that the Billy McCurrie she knew was the same man Jacqui had been praying for. 'How do you know all this stuff about him?' the girl enquired. Jacqui told her that the man Billy murdered had been her mum's fiancé.

Exactly forty years on from when she began praying for the salvation of a young murderer, Jacqui was able to get Pastor McCurrie's contact details. After a few emails back and forth, Billy was finally convinced that Jacqui was who she said. His uncertainty about her validity was because he had never been told that Desi had been in a relationship. Jacqui was able, via the internet, to watch some videos about Billy's story of how he became a Christian.

I learned that Billy's dad had been murdered by the IRA five years before he killed Desi and that he had been driven by unforgiveness and a strong desire for revenge. Eventually the time came when I was able to meet Billy face to face. I was invited to stay with him and his wife as I was due to attend a funeral nearby. I wasn't sure how my family would feel about it. As yet I hadn't told my mum or my sister about finding one of Desi's murderers, let alone that I was going to spend the night in his home! But I had peace in my heart about it so I accepted the invitation.

I was a bit anxious getting off my flight that day as Billy was picking me up from Liverpool Airport. From the videos I knew what he looked like but he had never even seen a photo of me. As I walked across towards him, I wondered what he was thinking. Then he realised it was me. We both extended our hands to shake them but within me it just felt right to give him a hug – after all I had been praying for him all those years and now he was my brother in Christ.

That night, while chatting at his home, I was able to ask some of the many questions I had regarding Desi. At the end we spent some time together in prayer at the kitchen table. It was surreal. I remember thinking, 'God, You are amazing! Only God could have done this.'

A few months later, when Billy came back to Northern Ireland to see his family, Jacqui arranged to meet up at his mum's house. That day Billy took her to see the memorial set up in memory of his murdered dad. Then, together, they took the very same route that he and his friend took that fateful morning when they murdered Desi. Jacqui recalls:

He showed me the street where they had been instructed to go to a house and collect two guns. Some of the information was very hard to listen to as we stood on the very spot where they had shot Desi in his car. The only question I could ask, the one question that had always been in my mind, was: 'Did you shoot him in the face?' Desi had been a very handsome man but as a twelve-year-old I had not been allowed to see him in his coffin or attend his funeral. I always wondered if his face had been touched by bullets that day. I had wondered if my mum had been able to see the love of her life one last time before he was buried. Billy assured me that although Desi had been shot numerous times, his face was untouched. The reason he knew that for certain was because there had been a mix-up with the solicitors. Desi's autopsy photographs had been sent to Billy's solicitor by mistake, so he had been able to see them while in prison.

Jacqui found out so many things about Desi from Billy that day; things she had never known before. The reason why Billy and his friend murdered Desi was because they had been told that he was an informant. However, the story that was told behind bars by men who were in the same UVF unit as Desi was completely different. It was not mistaken identity, nor was he an informant. Her mum later told her that Desi had received a letter prior to his murder saying that there were five bullets with his name on them, but he just laughed it off. Sadly he paid the price for that with his life. Jacqui also reveals:

BILLY – A FORMER TERRORIST

I have kept in contact with Billy. I pray that God will use him to reach young men in an effort to prevent them from joining gangs and making the same mistakes as he did. The very heart of Christianity is about forgiveness. When we repent, God forgives us, and He commands us to forgive others. From my own experience I know that this is not always easy but, with God's help, it is possible.

6

Myra and John – Truth Seekers

As human beings we are by nature truth-seekers; as
fallen human beings we are also by human nature
truth-twisters.

(Dr Os Guinness)[9]

Many and varied are the forms of religion which deceive sincere people looking for truth. Yet all false religions have the same flaws that reveal them to be imposters. The 'wolves' of false religion do not necessarily come looking like wolves but rather come in 'sheep's clothing' that appears to be 'real wool'. To discover that what you have believed in and followed for many years turns out to be false must seem devastating. A great hole is left inside the person that only truth can fill.

Myra met John when she was sixteen years old. Friendship blossomed, turning to love, so that by the time she was nineteen she was married. For their generation this was not thought unusual or uncommon. John had been trained at agricultural college in York. On graduating he was offered a managerial position looking after a demonstration poultry unit in Yorkshire of over 10,000 birds plus 3,000 day-old chicks. Many visitors travelled to this farm to see how flocks of poultry should be kept in ideal conditions. Myra and John were fortunate to be given a tied cottage – free accommodation that went with the job – on the estate where he worked. All those birds and visitors took some looking after but the newlyweds did not mind. Although they were extremely busy, they were also very happy. To their delight their son, Johnathan, was born, giving much joy and added responsibilities.

One Sunday morning there was a knock on the door. On the step stood a man, a stranger, who had taken the trouble to cycle all the way down their farm track especially to see them. Myra remembers exactly what he said: 'Do you believe in God?' He was a Jehovah's Witness, although Myra wasn't too sure what that meant. She had never heard of them. The man asked if they would like to have a Bible study each week. They agreed as they both felt that they did want to know more about God and the Bible. This was the start of their regular contact with the Jehovah's Witnesses (JWs).

In 1964 they moved to an area of Leeds where John was able to set up his own poultry unit. Their second son, Richard, came on the scene shortly afterwards to complete their family. Life was busy with plenty to do especially as there were further visits from the local JWs from the Kingdom Hall, their place of worship. Myra recalls:

I myself did not grow up in a Christian home. Both my mother and aunt were made to go to chapel twice on Sundays, as was the custom of their day. Mother always said that when she had her own children, she would not make them go to church ... so my brother and I never did go! But, strangely enough, even as a small child, and every night before I fell asleep, I used to say a little prayer.

Myra and John would discuss various things that had cropped up when being with the JWs. They would wonder what life was all about. You live for seventy years or more ... and then what? The JWs seemed to have all the answers. By now John and Myra had become fully involved to such an extent that it was their turn to go out doorknocking on the streets. Myra hated doing it, especially as she did not really know if the JWs had got it right.

John and I were still searching for the truth. We attended their conventions every year, held at the local major football stadium. I went to the Kingdom Hall on Sundays, and on Wednesdays attended a mid-week meeting to do role play and to learn how to speak to people on doors. I never took our boys along because I was uneasy about some of the things the JWs believed in. One of the leaders and other members kept asking us why we wouldn't get baptised. 'You know, we have the truth,' they kept on saying to us.

So the years passed but I was still confused, as was John. I was uncertain and unsure, not knowing who or what to believe, or if the JWs were right or wrong. We were still searching. We had always believed in God but had only known the JWs teaching, of which we had doubts.

While Myra was so concerned about what they should do, things changed quite dramatically. She had been praying that God would show her which way to go – stick with the JWs or ...? One day a friend of hers casually gave her some leaflets saying, 'These were given to me by some born-agains. You will be more interested than me.' She was also given the autobiography of a celebrity who had become a Christian. This was all new to Myra, never having met any of these Christians, but she felt that something was beginning to happen in her life as she read the leaflets.

By now her boys had grown up, so she decided to look for part-time work and ended up working in different supermarkets promoting goods. There were a lot of female colleagues with whom she got on well, so Myra was enjoying the busyness of her job. She then discovered that one of them was a Christian, a 'born-again'. Their friendship grew over lunch where Catherine explained from the Bible what a true Christian was and how to become one.

She would write down some verses from the Bible for me to look up when I got home. She also explained that I could get right with God by asking Jesus into my life. I was interested so we kept in touch.

One day the phone rang and it was Catherine, inviting me to go with her to church. They were having some special meetings that she thought I would enjoy. I gladly went along not knowing really what to expect. A young man was preaching from the Bible about trusting in Jesus Christ as Saviour and Lord. In the course of his sermon he had his arms outstretched, as Jesus would have done on the cross. At that moment it was as though the blinds had suddenly been removed from my eyes and I understood the glorious gospel of salvation.

It was only by grace, God's unmerited favour, that I could obtain the free gift of everlasting life. I realised that there was nothing I could do to earn my way to heaven. It was by grace not works, as I had been led to believe before. No amount of knocking on doors or doing whatever the Kingdom Hall said and did could get me right with God.

For it is by grace you have been saved, through faith – and this not from yourselves, it is the gift of God – not by works, so that no one can boast (Ephesians 2:8–9).

So that night, after all the confusion with the JWs and years of searching, I finally asked Jesus into my life to become my Lord and Saviour. I surrendered to Him to take control of my life, forgive my sins and make me a new person. And He did exactly what He promised.

How gracious he will be when you cry for help! As soon as he hears, he will answer you (Isaiah 30:19).

Christ died on the cross, bearing the punishment for my sins, then rose from the dead, triumphant over sin and death. All this was so that those who repent and believe in Jesus might enjoy eternal life with God forever.

There was a total change and difference in Myra's life. Her life was not problem-free, but inwardly her faith in Christ was growing, giving peace and assurance whereas before there had been only emptiness and confusion.

I walked free in the love of Jesus, and I still hold on to God's promise to be with me in this life and then for me to be with my Lord in eternity. I had been in fear and bondage with the JWs, whose teaching was proven to be false, but now I had been set free to enjoy God forever.

So perhaps you are wondering about John, her husband – what did he think and did he see changes in Myra? It was undeniable that something had happened. She was no longer anxious and confused. Instead she quietly and confidently lived out her faith before family, friends and neighbours, sharing what Jesus had done for her. One of her sons became a believer but John still kept searching. Friends were praying for him to understand and experience the truth that:

> God so loved the world that he gave his one and only Son, that whoever believes in him shall not perish but have eternal life (John 3:16).

> While on holiday with our son, we were all walking to church one Sunday evening as was our custom. But John, unknown to us, had quietly in his own heart been asking God to show him the way and the truth. Later he told us about this and what happened afterwards. He experienced something that he could not explain but could only describe as wonderful. He felt at peace. That night he asked Jesus to come into his life.

Jesus says:

> I am the way and the truth and the life. No one comes to the Father except through me (John 14:6).

Further Information

For further help for those involved in modern religious movements, please contact Tony Brown via his website www.cults-investigated.com

7

Ziggy – A Descendant of the Holocaust

[The Holocaust] The mass murder of Jews under the German Nazi regime during the period 1941–5. More than 6 million European Jews, as well as members of other persecuted groups, were murdered at concentration camps such as Auschwitz.

(Definition of holocaust in English: *OED*)

Ziggy had four Jewish grandparents. On his father's side were the less religious grandparents, rooted into the East End of London since the beginning of the twentieth century. Grandma, born in 1916 and a lifelong seamstress (as well as part-time pianist in the local cinema), was one of the last children of a large immigrant family who had travelled from Moldova to evade the pogroms both there and in Ukraine. The anti-Semitism had been so vile and violent that Grandma's father and brother came over to England to find work. When eventually they had saved up enough money, they brought their wives and children over as well. Grandpa, like Grandma, was born in the East End of London and in the same year. His family were Russian Jewish people, his father, Wolfe Rogoff, having fought and died in the First World War for England. No one knows much else about him although speculation arises as to why they have this very common Russian name. Grandpa became a carpenter. Ziggy remembers them as very warm people.

'My mother's side was a much more tragic story,' Ziggy sadly recalls. Her parents, Bubba and Zeida, were the more religious side of the family. Zeida came from a town near Warsaw in the early years of the twentieth century, with his mother, to live in England. A deal had been struck with a Jewish family that they would bring them over and Zeida would marry their daughter. What they had not told him was that his fiancée was disabled. The marriage did not last. He went on to fight for England in the First World War in a Jewish regiment in what was then Palestine.

'Bubba's story is the saddest of all,' Ziggy explains.

She came to England in 1939, arriving at Harwich with nothing, not even her suitcase which had been thrown out of a train window; her few clothes and precious photos were gone. She was twenty-six years old and lucky to have survived. Saying that she was a Christian during the interrogation saved her life. Her papers were forged.

Quite a lot of money would have been handed over on the black market to enable Bubba – and her sister – to escape from the country because Slovakia was about to become a disaster area for Jews. (At the last minute, though, Bubba's sister decided to stay, as she was in love with a dentist.) My grandmother eventually reached England after a week-long, arduous journey criss-crossing Europe, only to fall desperately ill on arrival in Harwich. She had left behind everything and everyone she ever knew. Now she was alone in a foreign land with a foreign tongue.

Upon recovery, Bubba took a position as a domestic assistant for a family in Liphook, Hampshire. As the family legend goes, on the first morning she was asked to cook bacon for them. Apologetically she informed the family that she was unable to do this because she was Jewish. The family's response was harsh. They said that they would make every effort to have her deported. She ran away that very night. She had met some Jewish people on a train once in England who told her that if ever she got into trouble, she should call the number that they gave her. Now was such a time. Her new friends helped her settle in the East End of London.

In retelling this story Ziggy explains that one has to see things from Bubba's narrow perspective, as she believed the family were Christians. The assumption being that if you were not Jewish, you must be Christian. This family clearly wasn't Jewish. Thus all her preconceived ideas about

Christians were reinforced by this terrible experience.

After World War Two Bubba married Zeida, a man twenty years her senior. During her honeymoon she received a telegram from Slovakia saying that there was no need to return to her homeland as none of her relatives had survived. All 885 residents of their town had been deported to Auschwitz concentration camp in Poland and none returned. Bubba had lost brothers, sisters, parents, her extended family and all her close friends; everyone she ever knew. Everybody had died. They had all been exterminated in the dreadful holocaust.

A memorial for the former residents was eventually constructed, including a mural painted by a famous artist, but later, when a communist government took control, it was flattened. Ziggy asked his mother if she herself ever commemorated the massacre. Apparently she used to take the day off work on the anniversary of her arrival in Harwich in 1939. That was her way of marking and remembering the atrocity. After the war Germany gave money back to Jewish people. Bubba wouldn't touch any of that 'blood money', as she called it.

Bubba's new friends helped her to settle in the East End of London, with Yiddish being her language. Ziggy's mother was born soon after Bubba's marriage, in her late thirties, as was another child who was born with severe mental difficulties and lived in a home until her passing. Bubba died in 2003 at the age of ninety in a care home for holocaust survivors.

ZIGGY – A DESCENDANT OF THE HOLOCAUST

Ziggy, born in 1970 and the eldest of two boys, was by his own admission a painfully shy boy. He freely admits that he led quite an insular life with little appetite for adventure beyond life at primary and then secondary school in Redbridge, Essex. Ziggy struggled with English, but he did very well with maths. Eventually, in later years, he obtained a first-class degree in mathematics from the University of Manchester, a masters and then completed his applied mathematics PhD at the University of Nottingham (his specialist subject being sound waves). A year of post-doctoral research in Russia was then followed by various avenues of work, including engineering in Lincoln, London, Deutsche Bank and Glencore, a commodity traders firm in Mayfair.

Ziggy recalls that even though he grew up in a Jewish household, the family never spoke about God but they had lots of traditions including observing food regulations, attending the synagogue and celebrating his Bar Mitzvah in Jerusalem.

But until I came to know a little about Christianity and what it said about a personal relationship with God, I would say that I would have considered God too distant to be known. He was too holy to be personally known. I used to think Jesus was a traitor to our people and had been rightly crucified as a blasphemer. At school I heard that Christians believed Jesus was the Messiah, but it only served to remind me that we were still waiting for the Messiah, and it wasn't Jesus.

91

My background is quite typical. Growing up, I would go to the synagogue on Friday nights as well as on the Sabbath morning (Saturday) in preparation for my Bar Mitzvah. This is the ceremony that Jewish boys take at the age of thirteen. They are then regarded as ready to observe religious precepts and take part in public worship. I would also go three times a week to Cheder, which is a traditional elementary school teaching the basics of Judaism and the Hebrew language. All the Jewish kids would congregate there, from the youngest of ages up until thirteen, then Jewish education ceases, unless they attend a specialised Jewish secondary school. My Bar Mitzvah was held at the Wailing Wall in Jerusalem as we were there for a month's holiday. If nothing else, it speaks of the pure Jewish identity of the family. I quite liked going to synagogue but as to the meaning of everything, I was unsure.

At university, life was different. There were opportunities to discuss, debate and discover what others think about all manner of issues. I met a guy who was neither Jewish nor Christian but we had a mutual Russian connection, which sealed our friendship. We used to discuss God. We were very wise in our own eyes and enjoyed ceremonially drinking shots of vodka Russian style as we explained how we saw our world: God was unknowable; God was distant; we didn't know Him. We were, I suppose, having fun intellectually but not really looking into any particular sect or engaging in anything. We were just interested in our own philosophy.

Then his friend became a Christian!

I had been abroad in Russia for a year, only to come back to find such a change in him. When he told all of us, our reaction was, 'Oh my goodness, it's like you've become weird. You've become like an alien. What have you done to yourself? You were perfectly normal one minute and now you are not! What are you doing? It makes no sense.'

I couldn't comprehend it. Still it was a great friendship. He was very kind and one of my very best friends, even today. Once or twice he invited me to a guest event at St Helen's Church, Bishopsgate in the City of London. I had never been into a church before so it felt strange going but yet safe because of the pure quality of our friendship. In terms of my work and things socially, not everything was going along as well as they could. I signed up to Christianity Explored, which is an informal course with meals that St Helen's runs where people like me could discuss and find answers to questions about faith, the Bible and Jesus.

There I met up with some lovely people. They seemed so different somehow to the people I normally encountered. I just loved those people and still do today. When they spoke to me about Jesus, I didn't want to brush it off like I would a spider off my neck. Perhaps I was thinking that since life wasn't going so well, this was a 'nice club' for me. But it could have been that I was thinking of the future, of having something in place in case anything bad happened. Or just maybe I needed to consider Jesus, even if only treating him like a big security blanket! Whatever the reason for my being there, the result was that I kept going back. I ended up reading Mark's Gospel, the second book in the New Testament, and genuinely thinking that Jesus could be the Messiah.

Finding himself with a period of peace and quiet in his life gave Ziggy the opportunity to reflect on what all this could mean. As he read the eyewitness accounts of the life, death and resurrection of Jesus, he discovered 'a Jesus I never could have imagined. He healed the sick. He raised the dead and even calmed the storm with a word.' Ziggy thought, 'Could this be the Messiah about whom I was told in the synagogue?' Soon he considered the cost of following Jesus as he reasoned with himself, 'How can I possibly think that Jesus is the Messiah if the Rabbis have been rejecting Him for two thousand years?'

Then someone passed on to him a book entitled *Betrayed!* by Stan Telchin, who was a successful American businessman and well-respected member of the synagogue and the Jewish community.[10] By the age of fifty Telchin had the enviable position of having obtained, by the world's standards, everything you could want. Then, out of the blue, his daughter rang home announcing that she had some sensitive news. Of course her parents were anxious as to what had happened. When they discovered that she had become a Christian, the family were outraged. They were devastated and felt betrayed. Didn't she know what the Christian church had done to the Jewish people?

Thinking that she had had some weird experience and had not really known what she was doing, her parents decided to read the New Testament for themselves in order to show her where she had gone wrong. Stan expected that it would read in the same vein as Adolf Hitler's *Mein Kampf* and was fully prepared to find some pretty horrendous stuff in it. 'I'll be able to show our daughter and we'll put this nonsense to rest!' he confidently asserted. To his utter surprise, he discovered that the Gospels are Jewish. Without spoiling the storyline too much, the whole family went on to become believers in Jesus. He wrote the book to help Jewish people understand that the most Jewish thing anyone can do is to believe in Jesus. He also opened up the many prophecies in the Hebrew Scriptures about the coming Messiah that point to Jesus, leaving readers no doubt that Jesus really is the Jewish Messiah.

At this point in his life, Ziggy found the book really helpful in overcoming what he calls his 'sententious angst'. He began to realise that he could believe in Jesus without relinquishing his Jewishness.

I got to the point where I believed in Jesus but didn't want to confess that He is the Messiah, the Saviour. I even compiled a list of 430 prophecies concerning the coming of the

Messiah in the Old Testament, including Isaiah 53, Psalm 22 and Daniel 9. These, along with others, are really great prophecies about who the Messiah was going to be, what He would look like and what He would do.

You can look back now and see that the Messiah is not just an ordinary man; He's divine. I found it so interesting. John 3 and Luke 24 show us that Jesus is the teacher of Israel as He explained the Hebrew Scriptures. The prophecies help us see that the Messiah was to be divine! Micah 5 plus Isaiah 11 and 53 teach us that He alone can lay down His life because He alone owns life.

It seems pretty straightforward. God has done everything He could to make it all abundantly clear, so that we can have no doubt that Jesus is the Messiah who has and will fulfil the prophecies.

Another book that Ziggy was encouraged to study was the New Testament book of Romans. This was written with Jewish people in mind, to help the Jewish believers in Rome understand that God's plan was to reach the whole world through the Jewish people and ultimately the Jewish Messiah, Yeshua. God was not the exclusive domain of Jewish people. Ziggy now understood that all people were the same before God but that the Jewish people were *the vehicle*, the nation that God made to bring His light into the world. Jesus, being fully divine and yet born a Jew, exactly fulfilled prophecy. He truly is *the* 'light of the world' (John 8:12).

But on 11 September 2001 that world was stunned when terrorists attacked the United States of America. Four planes were hijacked in mid-flight. Two of the planes were flown deliberately into the two skyscrapers at the World Trade Centre in New York City, causing them to catch fire and collapse, killing many hundreds of people. Around the world people were watching live coverage fearing and wondering if there would be another attack and where. Could this even be the beginning of an even greater catastrophe such as the end of the world? This wake-up call caused many to pray to, question, blame or deny their god. Ziggy, who had just returned from a Tuesday lunchtime talk at St Helen's to his office, was transfixed by what he was seeing on the TV screens. He says, 'I understood, at that moment, the reality that this world is fragile and how easily it can be destroyed.'

As well as digging into the Hebrew Scriptures himself, Ziggy was making new and lasting friends from St Helen's Church. On his first weekend away with the church he met Christians from many different ethnic groups, countries and even different religious backgrounds. They had all come together to worship the God of Israel, through His Son: the Messiah, Jesus. 'I looked at this room and knew in my heart that this is exactly what a promise to Abraham would look like: a blessing to many nations (Genesis 12:2).'

For Ziggy it was a moment of personal revelation that he knew he believed in Jesus. He realised that he had made an all-important life decision. He would follow Jesus. That very evening he attended Sunday church for the first time. His good friend who had first invited him to church rang him and said, 'You have some good news for me, haven't you?' Over a drink the following evening they encouraged each other in their new-found faith. Ziggy recalls:

> In that very first week I remember praying and being overwhelmed with two emotions: one was joy because I had found the Messiah, and the other was fear because I realised for the first time in my life that I had never honoured God's Son as my King, Creator and Sovereign Lord. I realised that I had lived my life my own way, with no regard to God or Jesus whatsoever.

He then began to be consciously aware of things he had done wrong in the past.

> I never thought about them being wrong before. Then I really began to be struck by my actions and by my attitude. I understood immediately that this is what the Bible means by the word 'sin'. It speaks of our wrong attitudes both to God and man. Sin cuts us off from God who is holy.

> Then I realised what Jesus had done for me. In the Old Testament part of the Bible it says:

> *... the Lord has laid on him the iniquity of us all*
> *(Isaiah 53:6).*

In a flash Ziggy realised that he had devoted so much energy into finding out if Jesus was the one that all Jews were waiting for, his *identity*, that he had almost overlooked Jesus' *mission*. Ziggy found himself asking the question, 'Why do we even need a Messiah?' The answer came quickly.

> *I understood that Jesus hadn't come just to heal the sick or raise the dead. He had come from heaven to earth to die for my sins, taking the punishment that I deserved. I was forgiven, not because of anything I had done, but because of what He had done. My heart was full of joy. God was real, and I knew Him and was forgiven by Him.*

Ziggy had experienced what happens when an individual does what is commanded of them: to repent and believe. He no longer believed that God was unknowable. Now he knew that God existed and he wanted to live *for* Him and *with* Him at the centre of his life.

> *No one has ever seen God; the only God, who is at the Father's side, he has made him known (John 1:18, ESV).*

> *The process of understanding Jesus as my Lord is ongoing. Without the fear of judgement but having respect and awe*

of His holiness, I am thankful to God for His great love for me, which brings great joy and peace to my heart.

Consideration of Jesus may be seen as the ultimate act of disloyalty for a Jewish person, but if Jesus is the promised Messiah, then to follow Him, believe in Him and indeed worship Him is the appropriate response – even in the enduring knowledge of the death of millions of my people in the Holocaust.

Further Information

Ziggy is married to Cristiana and they live in North London with their new baby Noah. He works with Jews for Jesus, helping Jewish communities understand who Jesus is.

If you would like to be in touch with him, please contact: ziggy@jewsforjesus.org

8

Alison Stewart – An Addict

You can argue with someone's opinion, but you can't argue with their story.

(Nicky Cruz)[11]

'By the age of three I had lived with six different sets of foster parents, finally settling with the seventh,' recounts Alison. This would not be the start that any of us would want for a child. She explains how this came about:

My foster parents were good people but, unknown to them, for many years my sister and I suffered sexual abuse by an older boy who came to live with us. Although I was a young girl, I was filled with guilt and shame, which was to pave a path for me. My older sister was the first to run away to try and find someone who could help us and stop what was happening. It wasn't long before social services came to ask me if the accusations were true. I was full of fear but told them that it was true, even though I was very much aware of the risk of losing my foster parents as a result. At this point I knew deep down inside that things wouldn't be the same again. I began to look for an opportunity to leave.

As a fifteen-year-old teenager, there came a day when Alison decided finally it was time to escape. She ran all the way to the streets of her capital city, Cardiff in Wales. There she encountered a totally different kind of world to that of the rural community in which she had grown up. With only the clothes that she stood up in, and with a bag in her hand, she appeared young, alone and vulnerable. When approached by an older man who offered to take her to his flat, she accepted naively what he offered. There she was introduced to the ways of criminality.

I didn't know anybody. I felt like a fish out of water. I wanted to belong. So I quickly adapted to this new kind of life. Within days I had been taught how to steal handbags and access people's accounts. I got a taste for this but deep down I just wanted to go home. After six months of chaos, I informed social services of my whereabouts, following which they came to get me. I was placed back into the care system, being pushed from home to home. I was so sad.

Following a spate of running away then being caught, a case conference was held where it was decided that she should be placed somewhere that was secure. Sixteen-year-old Alison, unable to help herself, was sectioned under the Mental Health Act into a secure mental institution where she battled for her sanity. While in there she witnessed upsetting scenes that scarred her emotionally. Each day she was assessed by a leading psychiatrist, an occupational therapist and a psychiatric counsellor.

I was told on a daily basis that I was mad and would never amount to anything. I realise now that words are very powerful. They have such an influential message. If you tell somebody something long enough, they will believe it in the end. I really believed that I was mad.

Alison was released eleven months later, deeply messed up as a person. She tried to live a normal life but failed. She lost every job she had. She failed with every relationship. Due to her unsettled state, she found herself running wild around the country. Some years later she met a man and fell in love but, as usual, nothing was straightforward for her. Unfortunately he introduced her to the hard-core drugs scene. Before she knew it, she was gripped and couldn't find any way out from its addictive clutches. At first she used cannabis but quickly escalated to heroin. It made her feel that she had found the answer. Initially it took her pain away. Her heart didn't hurt anymore as her emotions had been numbed. She was so 'high' that nothing really mattered. Before long she suddenly realised that she was seriously addicted to heroin and couldn't find a way to escape from it.

I remember waking up one morning thinking that I had a cold. As the day wore on, I went to the drug dealer's house where he gave me more heroin. The pain was gone. Then, in an awful moment, I knew that I was an addict. This drug had such a grip on me that, no matter what I tried to do, I could not break free. I went on every detox programme that society offered. I took all prescribed and non-prescribed pills. My doctor signed me in and I put myself into every hospital and institution that I could find, but nothing worked. I physically felt ... well, the only way I can describe it is that it was though a monkey was sitting on my back and I couldn't shake it off. It is a strange way to talk but that was how I felt.

For nine long years Alison struggled with her addiction, developing a minor crack habit. She was living in squalor, constantly being caught by the police for selling drugs. Because they were continually raiding her house and kicking in the doors so many times, she began living on the top floor of the house. Her windows were boarded up; the back door had no glass; there were no carpets on the floor; there was never any food in the cupboard. She confesses that she was living like a pig. A waif of only five and a half stone in weight, she was a sorry sight. Inwardly she felt that if only she could change her situation or do something different, then maybe life would be different. But no matter what she did or how hard she tried, nothing altered. It was not long before she found herself as a *Big Issue* seller on the streets of Newport, South Wales. She was broken and felt totally without hope.

When I was seventeen years old, I met a guy called Leroy. Having heard that I was in a mess, he came looking for me. I thank God for him. He took me to his home where he lovingly looked after me, bringing me back to life. He believed in me and helped me to come off all drugs. I remained drug-free for eighteen months, but I felt so empty inside. I couldn't understand how, after all that time, I should feel so lifeless. I used to sit and wonder, 'Why do I feel so empty?' I tried to fill my emptiness, the void within, by turning to alcohol. I would secretly drink downstairs where nobody could see me. I was trying to find peace; to find life. I wanted to find the answer but instead my life just grew sadder and sadder. Looking for love, I began a violent relationship which nearly killed me. One night he took me to his bedroom, which was covered in plastic, and he entered with an axe in his hand, threatening to chop me up with it. He put the axe to my foot and proceeded to tell me how he was going to remove my foot first and how he would then carry on. In that crazy moment I sat on the bed and looked at my fingertips that were black and yellow. I looked at my skinny body. I was in such a mess I thought, 'You can take my life.' But then something inside of me stirred and I began to fight for my life. The axe was put down but he kept beating me with a stick. I was beaten brutally within an inch of my life. The following day, in my friend's house, I began to haemorrhage from my nose and mouth. At the same time I felt something 'bad' enter the room. It is hard to describe. Fear gripped me with such a force that I knew death was upon me. At this point I sat down with a bucket on my lap, blood pouring down into it. Then, I can honestly say from the depth of my heart, I cried out my first ever real prayer to God: 'God, please don't let me die!' I had prayed prayers to God in the past, such as, 'God, get me out of this police station' or 'God, please don't let me get caught stealing today.' But this was a different prayer. This was something deep and very true from me, from my heart.

Her bleeding stopped. She did not acknowledge God but was thankful to be alive. The experience so shook her that she knew that if drugs didn't kill her, then surely this man would next time. She knew she had to find a different path for her life. That was when she met Bernie.

Bernie set up an interview for her with an organisation called Teen Challenge, a Christian rehabilitation centre in South Wales. Alison honestly admits that she was not interested particularly in finding God; she simply wanted to get 'clean'. She thought that if she could only get an opening, a break in life, then she would be alright. Putting her mind to doing so, she told friends that she would see them in six weeks when she came home, aiming to have another go at life. What she hadn't expected, two days into the programme, was how she would be touched by the incredible atmosphere of peace, love and acceptance in the place.

I was surrounded by many girls who had gone through similar experiences to mine but were beginning to break through. In the detox nurse's office I heard for the very first time in my life the good news, the message of Jesus Christ – who He is and why He came to earth.

God so loved the world that he gave his one and only Son, that whoever believes in him shall not perish but have eternal life (John 3:16).

With my head hung low and feeling totally broken, I listened intensely as the nurse told me about Jesus and how much He loves me. She told me how He could heal me and how He would forgive me. She explained that if I trusted in Him, repented and was genuinely sorry for the bad things I had done, then Jesus would come into my life and help me – if I asked Him to. To be honest, I had my back against the wall. I'd done everything, I'd seen everything, but nothing had worked. Then I began to cry. I remember sitting on the settee crying, not knowing how to pray, but this lady prayed and I repeated her words. I genuinely repented and asked God to heal me.

Although I didn't see any bright lights or anything dramatic, nor did I feel anything in particular, the next day I noticed

I was different. I should have been crawling up the walls, gasping for a cigarette and craving for a drink, but I wasn't and I knew that God must be real. For nine years I'd tried every possible way to find a cure but I hadn't. Now the monkey was off my back! I tell you, if you have been addicted to heroin and crack cocaine for nine years and all of a sudden it is gone, you know that God is real. I know He touched me. I no longer craved anything. I had a deep desire to read the Bible, which was crazy. I would go to my bedroom, get the Bible out and read as I was so hungry for it. I couldn't understand it all but the power of God's Word began to change me. It felt as though weights were coming off me. Better still, I felt clean inside where I had felt so rotten for years.

God's healing process had begun in Alison's life. With His love, and the love, care and support of those at Hope House, she began to experience the power of God in her life. He was changing her and she was developing a deep relationship with God through prayer, Bible reading and being with God's people. There had been a total transformation, both physically – as her body recovered and gained strength – and emotionally – as she found healing from her past hurts and childhood memories. Through finding the forgiveness of God, she was able to forgive those who had hurt her. A peace came into her life that no drug had ever brought her. Alison declares, 'Now I know the true meaning of living. I am free.'

> *For God did not send his Son into the world to condemn the world, but to save the world through him (John 3:17).*

After graduating from the programme, Alison has been used to help many find freedom from addiction and peace with God. However, becoming a Christian does not mean that there is automatic immunity from problems and struggles! Life can be often messy and it certainly has not been easy for Alison. She has had a failed marriage, which hurt deeply. But she knows God is with her as she lives for Jesus, as well as enthusiastically telling others that He can save completely those who come to Him.

Further Information

If you are trapped in an addiction and would like help for a way out please contact Teen Challenge:

Phone: 01664 822221 (an out-of-hours answerphone service is available)
Email: info@teenchallenge.org.uk
Address: Teen Challenge UK, Willoughby House, Station Road, Nottinghamshire LE14 3BH
Website: teenchallenge.org.uk

9

The Greatest Story Ever Told

The greatest story is a true one. It is unique. It affects every person who has ever lived, or will live or is alive today. It even became the title of an epic film, *The Greatest Story Ever Told*, directed by George Stevens and featuring a huge cast including many well-known actors. Its subject is Jesus Christ. Controversial, loved, hated or dangerous is how people might describe Him; many simply ignore Him, use His name as a swear word or even have never heard of Him. But Jesus once asked one of His followers, 'Who do men say that I am?' followed by 'Who do you say I am?'

Who Is Jesus?
For most people in secular Britain God is very much on the edge, or even off, the plate of their lives. And yet in each of the stories we have just read, there was a time when God became very real to them. The infinite God is an intimate God who we can know personally.

Born into poverty and obscurity, Jesus Christ was taken as a refugee to Egypt. He received no formal education, worked as a craftsman and never wrote a book or song. Jesus preached and ministered for only three years. He never spoke to flatter the authorities and refused to ever compromise His message. In those three years of public service, without travelling far, He made blind people see, the mute to speak and the deaf to hear. He healed lepers and lame people. He raised the dead back to life. He fed thousands of hungry people with just a few loaves and fishes. He calmed in an instant a rough storm at sea and walked on water, dispelling the fear of terrified fishermen.

Nobody spoke as Jesus did. He had authority. He gave to the world the highest moral standard, preaching only what He practised. Christ taught love your enemies; do good to those who hate you; bless those who curse you; pray for those who ill-treat you; and if someone strikes you on the cheek, turn the other.[12] Christ gave dignity to women, respect to the disabled, significance to children, esteem to the family and status to each individual. Christ has made an indelible impact on our literature, art, music and architecture, as well as our democratic freedoms.

At the age of thirty-three Jesus was executed by crucifixion. Judas Iscariot, who handed Him over to his enemies, cried, 'I have betrayed innocent blood.'[13] Pontius Pilate, the Roman Governor of that time, ordered His crucifixion but said, 'I find no basis for a charge against this man.'[14] The Roman centurion responsible for overseeing

Jesus' death reflected on Him saying, 'Surely this man was the Son of God!'[15]

It is impossible to fault Christ. He had no sin, nor did any wrong, for He was God 'manifested in the flesh'.[16] In Jesus God was made flesh and dwelt among us. Stripped naked, beaten and humiliated, Christ died. As He hung there on the cross, God laid on Jesus all the wrongdoing, the sin, of us all. Jesus took the punishment in our place that we might be forgiven for all our rebellion against God. Three days later the tomb where Jesus was laid was empty: He had physically risen from the dead. Over an extended period of time Jesus showed Himself alive to many people, before ascending back to heaven from whence He came.

But if Jesus rose from the dead, then He has done what no mere human ever could. The desire to dismiss the Bible record is not new. Journalist Frank Morrison set out to disprove Jesus' resurrection, only to end up writing a book entitled *Who Moved the Stone?*[17] which outlines the evidence for Jesus' rising from the dead. The historic evidence is overwhelming. Brilliant British historians and lawyers have examined the subject widely only to conclude that they are convinced that it is a fact of history. Among these are Professor Norman Anderson, Lord Denning (a former Master of the Rolls), and Lord Hailsham and Lord Mackay of Clashfern (both former Lord Chancellors), who have all spoken and written about their belief that the evidence for the resurrection is watertight. Acting Lord Chief Justice Charles Darling said of Jesus' resurrection, '... there exists such overwhelming evidence, positive and negative, factual and circumstantial, that no intelligent jury in the world could fail to bring in a verdict that the resurrection story is true.' Even Lew Wallace's 1880 novel *Ben-Hur: A Tale of The Christ*, which became a blockbuster film, was originally intended to disprove the story of Jesus. But after rigorously researching the subject and evidence, he became so convinced of the truth that he became a Christian and wrote his book.

So why did Jesus have to die? The greatest story ever told is one of rescue, forgiveness and freedom. God has made Himself known to the world He has made. He has revealed Himself to be a personal, just, loving and holy God. He has absolute power; He knows all things and is everywhere; He never changes. And yet God, who is a Spirit, clothed Himself in humanity as He came into our world to reach and rescue us. God the Creator became like His creation in the person of Jesus. As the merging of the colours blue and scarlet produces the colour purple, so too Jesus was the perfect bringing together of deity and humanity. He is fully God and fully human.

Out of love for us all, Jesus came from heaven to live among a world in rebellion against God. He became the substitute and sacrifice for our sin. God is bigger than and beyond time; He can see the past, present and future all at once. When Jesus was on the cross, God looked backwards in time to the first sin and forwards to the last sin, then took the wrong of all people and laid it on Christ. Jesus died carrying on Himself the sin of all wrong thinking, speaking and doing. Jesus suffered, bled and died so that we might be cleansed, forgiven and united with God, who loves us dearly.

In response Jesus calls us to turn from our sin and ask for forgiveness, trusting Him as our Lord and Saviour. As we do, by His Holy Spirit, He comes to live within us, helping us know Him more and to live for Him until the day God takes us to be with Him forever. Heaven is not a reward for our good deeds but a gift God offers to all, purchased by Jesus' death and resurrection.

No wonder this is the greatest story ever told!

Notes

Notes

1. D.J. Carswell, *Real Lives* (10Publishing, 2011).

2. Please note that original names in this story have been changed.

3. Head banging is self-harming as a way to cope with problems if anxious, stressed or depressed.

4. Please note that original names in this story have been changed.

5. Bilquis Sheikh, *I Dared To Call Him Father* (Chosen Books, 1978).

6. Christian Unions (CUs) are evangelical Christian student groups, often affiliated to their university's Student Union.

7. Stuart Burgess, *Hallmarks of Design: Evidence of Purposeful Design and Beauty in Creation* (DayOne, 2000).

8. '… all have sinned and fall short of the glory of God' (Romans 3:23).

9. Os Guinness, *Time for Truth* (Baker, 2002).

10. Stan Telchin, *Betrayed!* (Chosen Books, 1980).

11. Nicky Cruz, *The Devil Has No Mother* (Hodder & Stoughton, 2013).

12. This teaching can be found in Matthew 5:44; Luke 6:27–29.

13. Matthew 27:4.

14. Luke 23:4.

15. Mark 15:39.

16. 1 Timothy 3:16 (ESV).

17. Frank Morison, *Who Moved the Stone?* (Authentic, 2006).

Contacts

If you would like to know more about the Christian faith, the Bible, or find a church, please contact:

Web: www.10ofthose.com or www.tell-me-more.org

Email: roger@rogercarswell.com

Post: Life Stories, c/o Unit C, 10ofThose, Leyland, PR25 2DY

Further Reading

Roger Carswell, *Comfort in Times of Sorrow*
(10Publishing, 2012)

Roger Carswell, *Grill a Christian* (10Publishing, 2011)

D.J. Carswell, *Live Wires* (10Publishing 2011)

John Chapman, *Making the Most of the Rest of Your Life*
(Matthias Media, 2007)

Mark Ashton, *On My Way To Heaven* (10Publishing, 2010)

D.J. Carswell, *Real Lives* (10Publishing, 2010)

Roger Carswell, *Where is God in a Messed-up World?*
(IVP, 2009)

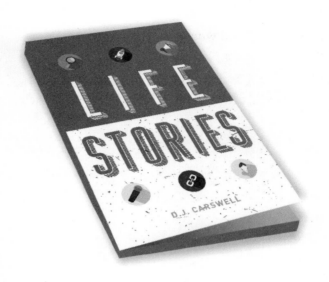

10Publishing is the publishing house of 10ofThose. It is committed to producing quality Christian resources that are biblical and accessible.

www.10ofthose.com is our online retail arm selling thousands of quality books at discounted prices.

For information contact: info@10ofthose.com or check out our website: www.10ofthose.com